Retirement Fun for Retirees:

Celebrating Life Off the Clock with Bold Adventures, Spirited Laughter, and Hundreds of Ideas for Unforgettable Moments of Freedom and Joy

By:
Jorvik Vale

© **Copyright 2024 - All rights reserved.**

The contents of this book may not be reproduced, duplicated, or transmitted without the direct written permission of the author or publisher.

Under no circumstances will the publisher or author be held liable for any damages, recovery, or financial loss due to the information contained in this book. Neither directly nor indirectly.

Legal Notice:

This book is protected by copyright. This book is for personal use only. You may not modify, distribute, sell, use, quote, or paraphrase any part or content of this book without the permission of the author or publisher.

Disclaimer Notice:

Please note that the information contained in this document is for educational and entertainment purposes only. Every effort has been made to present accurate, current, reliable, and complete information. No warranties of any kind are stated or implied. The reader acknowledges that the author is not offering legal, financial, medical, or professional advice. The contents of this book have been taken from various sources. Please consult a licensed professional before attempting any of the techniques described in this book.

By reading this document, the reader agrees that under no circumstances will the author be liable for any direct or indirect loss arising from the use of the information contained in this document, including but not limited to - errors, omissions, or inaccuracies.

Table of Contents

Table of Contents 3

Chapter 1 Welcome to Your New Lifestyle 5

- Introduction: Description of the target audience 5
- Setting the tone for the book 7

Chapter 2 Setting Goals and Mindset for Retirement 9

- Defining Your Retirement Goals 9
- Identifying personal objectives and desires 10
- The importance of having a sense of purpose 12
- Developing a Positive Retirement Mindset 13
- Embracing change and new beginnings 15
- Overcoming common fears and misconceptions about retirement 16

Chapter 3 The Game of Retired Life – And How You Play It 19

- Crafting Your Daily Action Plan 19
- Balancing routine and spontaneity 21
- Creating lists of activities to consider 22
- Incorporating variety and excitement into your daily life 23

Chapter 4: Travel Adventures 26

- Discussing the benefits of travel in retirement 26
- Overcoming travel challenges and concerns 28
- Listing exciting travel destinations 30
- Tips and resources for planning trips 31

Chapter 5 Home Sweet Home 34

- Transforming your living space into a haven 34
- Decluttering and embracing minimalism 36
- Exploring hobbies and activities you can enjoy at home 38

Chapter 6 Embracing the Great Outdoors 42

- Benefits of outdoor activities for physical health 42
- Incorporating outdoor exercise into your routine 44
- Birdwatching, hiking, and other nature-focused activities 47
- Finding solace and joy in the natural world 49

Chapter 7 Fitness for Life 51

- Discussing the significance of staying physically active 51
- Different types of exercise and their benefits 55
- Tailoring fitness activities to your interests 58
- Making exercise an enjoyable part of your daily life 60

Chapter 8 Nourishing the Soul 64

- Exploring the importance of mental health in retirement 64
- Mindfulness, meditation, and their benefits 66
- Practicing mindfulness in everyday activities 69
- Finding inspiration through reading and self-reflection 71

Chapter 9 Connecting with Others 74

- Strategies for making new friends and strengthening existing connections 74
- The role of social engagement in retirement 77
- The benefits of community involvement and volunteer work 79
- Identifying opportunities to contribute to society 81

Chapter 10 Crafting Your Retirement Legacy 84

- Reflecting on your life's purpose and legacy 84
- How to create a meaningful retirement legacy? 86

Conclusion: Keep the Fun Rolling 89

Appendix: Lists of Activities and Resources 90

Chapter 1
Welcome to Your New Lifestyle

- **Introduction: Description of the target audience**

Welcome to a new phase of life, where the daily grind is in the rearview mirror, and the horizon is painted with the hues of endless possibilities. If you're holding this book in your hands, or perhaps scrolling through these pages, it's likely because you're standing at the crossroads of retirement, or you've already embarked on this thrilling journey.

Meet the Adventurers

In these pages, we won't lecture you about what retirement should be. We won't tell you what to do, and we certainly won't prescribe a one-size-fits-all formula for happiness. What we will do is take a moment to introduce you to your fellow adventurers in this exciting chapter of life.

Newly Retired Dreamers

Some of you may have recently bid farewell to the workforce, eager to savor the sweet fruits of your labor. You're looking for inspiration, for a way to break free from the routine that once defined your days. You've hit the pause button on your career, but you're nowhere near ready to hit pause on life itself.

Explorers of the Unseen

Among you are those who have longed for the day when time would be your ally, not your adversary. You're seeking interesting ideas and fresh possibilities that ignite your passion and curiosity. Retirement, to you, is an opportunity to rewrite the script, to explore the world with newfound zeal, and to dive headfirst into the uncharted waters of your interests.

The Quest for Renewal

For some, retirement is a ticket to a fresh start—a chance to design your days from scratch. You're on a quest to uncover hidden talents, unearth latent passions, and discover the joy in the simplest of moments. You understand that retirement is not a destination but a thrilling journey filled with untapped potential.

A Lifelong Pursuit of Fun

In this book, we will delve into the art of crafting your retirement with purpose and enthusiasm. The objective is clear: "Enjoy yourself, it's later than you think." Together, we'll navigate the labyrinth of this new chapter, using your time wisely to accomplish the goals you have in mind. Let the universe become your partner in creating a present and future that sparkles with fulfillment.

Who Should Read This?

If you're looking to avert the dreaded boredom that sometimes lurks in retirement's shadows, yearning for new connections, constructive interests, and hobbies that stimulate your mind, body, and soul, then you've come to the right place.

We understand that retirement is not just about postponing mortality through longevity; it's about embracing a positive mindset and seizing every moment to do the things that bring you joy. Whether you've retired early, by choice, or due to circumstances, this book is your guide to living a life that's vibrant, fulfilling, and filled with fun.

A Word on What You Won't Find Here

Before we embark on this adventure together, let's set a few expectations straight. You won't find cliché senior jokes, derogatory remarks about retirement, or tired bucket lists within these pages. Instead, we're here to explore engaging and mindful activities—simple and beautiful things that enhance your life, stimulate your mind, and boost your longevity and health.

This book is a celebration of life, a testament to the joys that await you in your retirement years. So, whether you're a recent retiree, someone with newfound freedom, or a friend or family member looking to gift this book to a retiree, welcome to a world of possibilities and the pursuit of "Retirement Fun in 2024." Let's dive in and start creating your unique retirement adventure.

- **Setting the tone for the book**

As you embark on this journey through the pages of "Retirement Fun in 2024," it's essential to set the right tone. Retirement, for many, marks the transition from a structured and often demanding working life into a chapter where time becomes a treasured commodity. But it's far more than that—it's a journey of rediscovery, of unearthing passions, and of embracing life's abundant offerings.

In these chapters, we won't dwell on the conventional stereotypes of retirement—those images of endless leisure, idle days, or even the notion of a 'bucket list.' Instead, we're going to dive into a world where retirement is not about slowing down, but about speeding up the pursuit of your dreams.

The Symphony of Possibilities

Picture retirement as a vast symphony, with each day offering a different note, a unique melody. Your role as the conductor of this symphony is to orchestrate your days, creating harmonies of joy, adventure, and fulfillment. Whether you're newly retired, anticipating retirement on the horizon, or have experienced it for some time, the possibilities that lie ahead are boundless.

A Guide, Not a Rulebook

This book is your guide to navigating this intricate composition. It's not a rulebook or a rigid set of instructions. Instead, it's a companion—a trusted friend that walks beside you as you uncover the gems of retirement. It's about helping you design your own unique masterpiece, one day at a time.

An Invitation to Fun

We're here to celebrate life in all its vibrant hues. To encourage you to embrace new experiences, learn new things, and create unforgettable memories. Retirement is not a destination but a thrilling journey filled with twists and turns, surprises, and serendipities. It's an opportunity to explore, grow, and enjoy every moment to its fullest.

So, as you turn the pages of this book, imagine that you're opening the door to a world of possibilities. A world where age is just a number, and your enthusiasm is the compass guiding you through uncharted territories. We'll explore, learn, and have fun along the way, and together, we'll make the most of this remarkable chapter in your life. Welcome to the adventure that is "Retirement Fun in 2024."

Chapter 2
Setting Goals and Mindset for Retirement

- **Defining Your Retirement Goals**

In this section, we delve into the heart of your retirement aspirations. It's about identifying the specific objectives that will shape your retirement experience.

Clarity and Purpose

Retirement is your canvas, and goals are the brushstrokes that bring it to life. They provide clarity and purpose to this new phase of your life.

Tailored Ambitions

Your retirement goals are highly personal, reflecting your passions, values, and dreams. They can encompass a wide range of interests, from travel and adventure to personal growth and contribution to society.

Reflection and Insight

We'll guide you through a process of reflection and self-discovery to uncover the goals that resonate most with you. This is not about what society expects; it's about what genuinely matters to you.

Short and Long-Term Vision

In this section, we address both short-term and long-term goals, ensuring that you have a well-rounded perspective on your retirement ambitions.

Balancing Dreams and Resources

While dreams are boundless, we also acknowledge the practical side of goal-setting. We help you align your aspirations with your financial means.

The Precision of SMART Goals

We emphasize the importance of setting Specific, Measurable, Achievable, Relevant, and Time-bound (SMART) goals, as they are more likely to be realized.

A Vision Takes Shape

By the end of this section, you will not only have goals but a vivid retirement vision—a clear picture of what you want to achieve, experience, and create in the years ahead. Your retirement will be defined by the goals that resonate deeply with you, making your journey uniquely meaningful.

- **Identifying personal objectives and desires**

Retirement marks a significant turning point in your life—a moment to rediscover, reevaluate, and recalibrate. It's about creating a future that reflects your innermost desires and personal objectives.

What Are Your Retirement Goals?

Retirement goals are the facets of life you wish to explore, experience, or achieve during your retirement years. These can encompass a wide spectrum of interests, from lifelong dreams to newfound passions.

Getting to Know Yourself

Begin this journey by looking within. What activities, experiences, or achievements have always sparked your interest or curiosity? What passions or hobbies have you set aside due to the demands of daily life?

Reflecting on Your Values

Consider your values and principles. What matters most to you in life? Is it family, adventure, personal growth, contributing to society, or simply finding contentment in the present moment?

Short and Long-Term Dreams

Your retirement canvas spans not just the immediate future but the years ahead. What are your short-term objectives, the things you'd like to achieve or experience in the next year or two? Equally, what are your long-term dreams that may unfold over the next decade or more?

Balancing Dreams and Reality

While dreams are boundless, it's crucial to consider the practical aspects. Take into account your financial situation, health, and other responsibilities. How can your goals align with your current resources and circumstances?

The Power of Specificity

Precise goals are more likely to be realized. Instead of vague notions, define your objectives in clear and specific terms. For instance, rather than saying, "I want to travel more," you might say, "I aim to visit five new countries within the next five years."

Documenting Your Goals

Consider writing down your goals. There's something powerful about putting pen to paper or typing them out. It makes them tangible and serves as a constant reminder of what you're working towards.

Discussing Your Goals

Don't hesitate to discuss your retirement goals with a trusted friend, partner, or advisor. They can provide insights, encouragement, and perhaps even ideas you haven't considered.

This process is about authenticity—discovering what truly resonates with you. It's your opportunity to sculpt a retirement that reflects your desires, values, and aspirations. By identifying your personal objectives and desires, you're taking the first step toward making your retirement vision a reality.

- **The importance of having a sense of purpose**

In the realm of retirement, the concept of a "sense of purpose" shines as a guiding star, illuminating the path to a fulfilling and meaningful life in this new chapter.

Fulfillment Beyond Leisure

Retirement is often portrayed as a time of leisure and relaxation. While relaxation has its merits, a sense of purpose goes beyond mere rest. It's the heartbeat of a rich and rewarding retirement.

A Reason to Wake Up Each Day

Imagine waking up in the morning with a clear sense of why your day matters. Having a purpose in retirement provides you with that reason. It's the motivation that propels you out of bed with enthusiasm.

A Lifelong Pursuit

A sense of purpose isn't something that's only relevant in your working years. In fact, it becomes even more vital in retirement. It's a lifelong pursuit of goals and aspirations that fuel your passion and drive.

Physical and Mental Wellbeing

Research has shown that individuals with a sense of purpose tend to enjoy better physical and mental health. They are more resilient, experience lower levels of stress, and have a higher overall quality of life.

A Fountain of Youth

In many ways, a sense of purpose can be your fountain of youth. It keeps you engaged, mentally sharp, and physically active. Retirement becomes a time of renewal rather than stagnation.

Connection to Others

A purpose often involves connecting with others. Whether through volunteer work, pursuing shared interests, or contributing to a cause, a sense of purpose can foster meaningful relationships and a sense of belonging.

Personal Growth and Achievement

Your sense of purpose can be a catalyst for personal growth and achievement. It's the driving force behind learning new skills, embracing challenges, and accomplishing your goals.

Defining Your Purpose

Your sense of purpose in retirement is deeply personal. It may revolve around family, community, personal hobbies, or a newfound passion. It could be as simple as cultivating a beautiful garden or as ambitious as starting a new venture.

Adapting and Evolving

Your purpose isn't static. It can evolve over time as your interests change or as new opportunities emerge. The beauty of retirement is that it allows you the freedom to explore and adapt your purpose as you see fit.

As we explore the depths of retirement, remember that a sense of purpose is not just a concept; it's the heartbeat of a fulfilling life. It gives your days meaning, keeps you engaged, and fosters wellbeing. It's your North Star, guiding you towards a retirement that's not just about relaxation but about vibrant, purpose-driven living.

- ## Developing a Positive Retirement Mindset

Retirement isn't just a change in your daily routine; it's a profound shift in perspective and lifestyle. Cultivating a positive retirement mindset is the cornerstone for embracing this new phase with enthusiasm, resilience, and joy.

The Power of Mindset

Your mindset shapes your reality. A positive retirement mindset isn't about avoiding challenges or difficulties; it's about facing them with optimism and adaptability.

Embracing Change

Retirement brings change, and change can be unsettling. But a positive mindset reframes change as an opportunity for growth, exploration, and reinvention.

Retirement as a New Beginning

Rather than viewing retirement as an endpoint, see it as a fresh beginning—a canvas waiting for you to paint your dreams, aspirations, and experiences.

Overcoming Retirement Myths

Let's debunk common myths about retirement. It's not a one-size-fits-all concept, nor is it solely a time for leisure. A positive retirement mindset embraces the diversity of experiences and aspirations.

Adopting a Growth Mindset

A growth mindset is the belief that abilities and intelligence can be developed with effort and learning. In retirement, it's about continually seeking new challenges and opportunities for personal growth.

Finding Purpose in Everyday Moments

A positive retirement mindset uncovers purpose in the ordinary. Whether it's enjoying a quiet morning coffee, tending to your garden, or reading a book, these small moments contribute to a fulfilling retirement.

Staying Open to New Experiences

An open mindset is receptive to new experiences and ideas. It's about saying "yes" to opportunities, whether it's learning a new skill, trying a new hobby, or embarking on an adventure.

Nurturing Resilience

Retirement, like life, has its ups and downs. A positive mindset fosters resilience—the ability to bounce back from setbacks, learn from challenges, and adapt to new circumstances.

Building a Supportive Network

Surrounding yourself with positive influences is crucial. Seek out friends, mentors, or support groups that align with your retirement aspirations and values.

The Art of Gratitude

A positive retirement mindset embraces gratitude. It's about appreciating the present moment, valuing your achievements, and acknowledging the blessings in your life.

Your retirement journey is a reflection of your mindset. Cultivating a positive retirement mindset is not just about thinking happy thoughts; it's about approaching this phase with intention, resilience, and a zest for life. As you navigate this new beginning, remember that your mindset is the compass guiding you towards a retirement filled with positivity, growth, and fulfillment.

- **Embracing change and new beginnings**

Change is the heartbeat of life, and retirement is a profound transition that beckons change and new beginnings. In this chapter, we explore the art of welcoming change with open arms and embracing the fresh opportunities it brings.

Change: The Only Constant

Change is an integral part of existence, and retirement is no exception. It's a time when the familiar rhythms of work life evolve into something new and uncharted.

Navigating Life Transitions

Retirement is not just an end; it's a doorway to new possibilities. It's a chance to redefine your purpose, your interests, and your daily routines.

Letting Go of the Past

Embracing change often involves letting go of certain aspects of your previous life—your work identity, routines, or roles. It can be a bittersweet process, but it opens space for fresh experiences.

The Power of Adaptability

Adaptability is a key trait in navigating change successfully. It's about being open to new ideas, willing to learn, and agile in the face of challenges.

Retirement as a Fresh Canvas

Retirement offers you a fresh canvas upon which you can paint the life you've always wanted. It's an opportunity for reinvention and exploration.

Finding New Passions

With change comes the chance to discover new passions. Whether it's a hobby you've always wanted to try, a skill you've wanted to master, or an interest you've yet to explore, retirement is the perfect time to dive in.

Creating New Rituals

Change doesn't mean abandoning your routines; it's about crafting new rituals that align with your retirement aspirations. These rituals can infuse your days with meaning and purpose.

Resilience in the Face of Change

Resilience is your ally in embracing change. It's the ability to bounce back from setbacks, learn from experiences, and continue forward with strength and determination.

New Beginnings as a Mindset

Embracing new beginnings is not just a phase; it's a mindset. It's about approaching each day with curiosity, a willingness to adapt, and an open heart.

Change is the thread that weaves the fabric of your retirement journey. Embracing change and welcoming new beginnings is not about erasing the past but embracing the future. It's about recognizing that your retirement years are an opportunity to craft a life filled with growth, discovery, and fresh experiences. As you navigate this chapter, remember that change is not the end—it's the beginning of something beautiful and exciting.

- **Overcoming common fears and misconceptions about retirement**

Retirement often stirs a cocktail of apprehensions and misconceptions. Here, we address these concerns directly, providing clarity and a realistic perspective on retirement.

Fear of the Unknown

The uncertainty that retirement brings can be intimidating. However, it's essential to remember that retirement also holds the promise of exciting new experiences and opportunities.

Financial Anxiety

Financial worries can cast a long shadow over retirement plans. By establishing a sound financial strategy and seeking professional advice, you can navigate this challenge with confidence.

Loss of Identity

The tie between one's identity and their career can be strong. While retirement may entail a shift in identity, it can also be an opportunity for self-discovery and exploring new dimensions of who you are.

Boredom and Inactivity

The misconception that retirement equates to idleness is far from the truth. It's a time to engage in activities that truly resonate with you, infusing your days with purpose and fulfillment.

Health Concerns

Prioritizing health is vital in retirement. Regular exercise, a balanced diet, and mental stimulation can help you maintain good health and vitality.

Loneliness and Isolation

Retirement can sometimes lead to feelings of isolation, but it's also a chance to nurture existing relationships and form new connections within your community.

Lack of Purpose

Retirement can offer a profound sense of purpose when you set meaningful goals and pursue activities that align with your values and interests.

The Myth of Age

Retirement isn't synonymous with old age. It's a stage of life where you have the freedom to pursue your passions, irrespective of age.

Changing Roles and Relationships

Retirement can indeed reshape family dynamics, but it can also be an opportunity to strengthen bonds and explore new roles within your family and community.

The Reality of Retirement

Retirement is as diverse as the individuals experiencing it. By addressing these fears and misconceptions, you can approach retirement with a clear understanding of its possibilities and challenges, ready to embrace this new chapter with open arms.

Chapter 3
The Game of Retired Life – And How You Play It

- **Crafting Your Daily Action Plan**

Retirement gifts you the freedom to design your daily life as you see fit. Here, we explore practical strategies for structuring your days to maximize this newfound freedom.

Balancing Freedom and Routine

In retirement, you have the luxury of time without the constraints of a nine-to-five schedule. However, some level of routine can provide structure and purpose to your days. Finding the right balance between spontaneity and structure is key.

Set a Morning Routine

Your morning sets the tone for the day. Consider creating a morning routine that aligns with your goals and preferences. It might involve exercise, meditation, reading, or simply enjoying a leisurely breakfast. A well-crafted morning routine can enhance your overall well-being.

Prioritize Your Priorities

Identifying your daily priorities ensures that you're consistently working towards your goals. These priorities can range from pursuing a passion project to spending quality time with loved ones. By focusing on what truly matters to you, your days become more purposeful.

Incorporate Passion Projects

Retirement is an excellent time to dive into hobbies and interests that bring you joy. Dedicate a portion of your day to these passion projects. Whether it's painting, gardening, or learning a new language, these activities add depth and fulfillment to your retirement.

Nurture Relationships

With more free time, you can strengthen your relationships. Schedule regular interactions with family and friends, and consider joining social groups or clubs that align with your interests. Meaningful connections contribute to a fulfilling retirement.

Mindful Moments

Incorporating mindfulness practices into your daily routine can promote mental and emotional well-being. Whether through meditation, deep breathing exercises, or mindful walks, these moments of presence can reduce stress and enhance your overall quality of life.

Reflect and Appreciate

Taking time to reflect on your day can offer valuable insights and a sense of accomplishment. Consider keeping a journal or engaging in reflective practices that allow you to appreciate your experiences and growth.

Flexibility and Spontaneity

While structure is beneficial, don't forget to leave room for spontaneity. Embrace unexpected opportunities and be open to trying new things. This flexibility adds a sense of adventure and serendipity to your retirement.

Stay Physically Active

Physical activity is crucial for maintaining health and vitality. Incorporate regular exercise into your daily routine. Whether it's walking, yoga, or fitness classes, staying active ensures you can fully enjoy your retirement years.

Cultivate Lifelong Learning

Retirement offers the perfect opportunity for continuous learning. Allocate time to read, take courses, or explore new skills. Lifelong learning not only keeps your mind engaged but also opens doors to new interests and experiences.

By applying these practical strategies, you can create a daily routine that reflects your values and aspirations in retirement. Your days become a canvas upon which you paint a fulfilling and purposeful life, rich with experiences, connections, and personal growth.

- **Balancing routine and spontaneity**

Retirement, the long-awaited phase of life where the shackles of the daily grind are finally shed, opens up a world of endless possibilities. It's a time to bask in the newfound freedom and embark on adventures that might have been postponed during the working years. In this section, we delve into the art of balancing routine and spontaneity to make the most of your retirement years.

Routine: Your Steady Anchor

Routines are the threads that weave the fabric of our lives. They offer a sense of predictability and comfort. In retirement, your routine can be a dependable anchor, grounding you as you navigate this new chapter.

Consider preserving certain aspects of your pre-retirement routine that bring you joy and purpose. Maybe it's the ritual of brewing your morning coffee and reading the newspaper or going for a daily walk in your favorite park. These familiar activities can provide structure to your day and maintain a sense of continuity.

However, the beauty of retirement lies in your ability to mold your routine to your liking. You're no longer bound by the clock or the demands of a job. You can choose when to wake up, how to structure your day, and what activities to incorporate into your routine. It's a blank canvas, and you're the artist.

Spontaneity: Embrace the Unexpected

Spontaneity injects a sense of excitement and unpredictability into your retired life. It's the joy of waking up with no fixed plans and the freedom to say "yes" to whatever the day brings.

When opportunities arise, whether it's a last-minute invitation from friends, a chance to explore a new hobby, or an impromptu road trip, seize them with enthusiasm. Spontaneous decisions often lead to some of the most memorable experiences in retirement.

Don't be afraid to deviate from your routine occasionally to embrace these spontaneous moments. They can reignite your sense of wonder and remind you that retirement is a time to savor life's unexpected pleasures.

Harmony: Crafting Your Ideal Retirement

Finding the perfect equilibrium between routine and spontaneity is a personal journey. It requires self-awareness and the flexibility to adapt as your preferences evolve. Some days, you may yearn for the comfort of a structured routine, while on others, the allure of spontaneity might be too enticing to resist.

Remember, retirement is an opportunity to craft a life that suits you best. Embrace the freedom to determine the degree of structure in your days. Balancing routine and spontaneity will enable you to make the most of each moment, ensuring that your retirement years are as vibrant and fulfilling as you've always imagined.

- **Creating lists of activities to consider**

In retirement, the canvas of your life is blank, waiting for you to paint it with vibrant strokes of experiences and adventures. To ensure that your retirement years are filled with fulfillment and purpose, one invaluable tool you can use is creating lists of activities to consider. These lists serve as a guide to help you explore new horizons and make the most of this exciting chapter.

1. Hobbies and Interests:

Start by reflecting on your passions and interests. Retirement is the perfect time to dive deeper into activities you've always wanted to pursue. Here are some ideas to consider:

- **Artistic Pursuits:** If you've ever been drawn to painting, sculpting, photography, or any form of creative expression, now is the time to explore your artistic side. Sign up for classes, invest in quality materials, and create your own masterpieces.
- **Gardening:** Cultivating a garden can be a therapeutic and rewarding hobby. Whether you have a green thumb or are a novice gardener, tending to plants and watching them flourish can bring immense joy.
- **Musical Endeavors:** Dust off that old guitar or piano, or pick up a new instrument you've always wanted to learn. Music has the power to soothe the soul and ignite creativity.
- **Culinary Adventures:** Cooking can be both an art and a passion. Experiment with new recipes, take cooking classes, or explore different cuisines from around the world.
- **Literary Exploration:** Dive into the world of books. Create a reading list of classic novels, explore different genres, or even try your hand at writing your own stories or memoirs.

2. Travel Destinations:

Retirement provides the freedom to explore the world at your own pace. Make a list of destinations you've always dreamt of visiting. Consider the following:

- **Local Exploration:** Start with places in your own region that you may have overlooked during your working years. Visit historical landmarks, nature reserves, or charming small towns nearby.
- **National Treasures:** Plan road trips or flights to explore the diverse landscapes and cultures within your own country. National parks, scenic drives, and cultural festivals await your discovery.
- **International Adventures:** If you've dreamt of exploring far-off lands, compile a list of international destinations that pique your interest. Research their history, culture, and cuisine to immerse yourself fully in the experience.

3. Volunteering and Giving Back:

Retirement can also be a time to give back to your community or a cause that resonates with you. Create a list of organizations or initiatives you'd like to get involved with:

- **Local Charities:** Find local charities or non-profits that align with your values. Whether it's mentoring youth, assisting the elderly, or supporting environmental initiatives, volunteering can be deeply fulfilling.
- **Skills-Based Volunteering:** Consider how your skills and expertise can be of service. If you have a background in finance, for instance, you could offer financial literacy workshops.
- **Global Outreach:** Explore opportunities for international volunteering or contributing to global causes that matter to you.

Creating these lists of activities to consider in retirement is not only a practical exercise but also an exciting one. It allows you to visualize the endless possibilities that await and serves as a constant source of inspiration as you navigate this new chapter in your life.

- **Incorporating variety and excitement into your daily life**

Retirement offers an opportunity to break free from the daily grind and infuse your life with a renewed sense of vitality. It's a time to embrace variety and excitement as you explore uncharted territory in your daily routines.

1. Morning Rituals with a Twist:

Start your day with a dash of novelty. Consider switching up your morning routine by trying a new breakfast recipe, practicing morning meditation, or taking a different route for your daily walk. Small changes like these can set a fresh tone for the day.

2. Thematic Days:

Dedicate certain days of the week to specific themes or activities. For instance:

- **Adventure Tuesdays:** Use Tuesdays for spontaneous day trips, exploring nearby hiking trails, or discovering hidden gems in your town.
- **Cultural Thursdays:** Explore a different aspect of culture each Thursday, whether it's trying international cuisine, attending a local art exhibit, or immersing yourself in a foreign film.

3. Pursue Lifelong Learning:

Stimulate your mind by enrolling in classes or workshops that pique your interest. Consider subjects like history, science, art, or even cooking. Learning something new not only keeps your brain engaged but also opens doors to exciting experiences.

4. Connect with Nature:

Nature is a constant source of wonder. Vary your outdoor experiences by:

- **Seasonal Adventures:** Embrace each season by engaging in activities that suit the weather. From gardening in spring to snowshoeing in winter, nature offers an ever-changing backdrop.
- **Birdwatching:** Explore the avian world by identifying local bird species. Create a checklist and seek out different birds in your area.

5. Socialize Creatively:

Diversify your social interactions by:

- **Themed Gatherings:** Host themed gatherings or potlucks with friends and family. Each gathering can revolve around a different theme, from international cuisine nights to classic movie marathons.

- **Meetup Groups:** Join local meetup groups or clubs that align with your interests. Whether it's a photography club or a book club, these gatherings introduce you to new people and activities.

6. Spontaneous Adventures:

Keep a list of nearby destinations or activities that you can explore at a moment's notice. When the mood strikes, embark on a spontaneous adventure, whether it's a day at the beach, a visit to a local museum, or a scenic drive to a neighboring town.

7. Exercise and Wellness:

Stay active and maintain a healthy lifestyle. Try different forms of exercise, from yoga to dance classes. Explore meditation, tai chi, or other wellness practices to invigorate your body and mind.

8. Creative Pursuits:

Nurture your creative side with a variety of artistic endeavors. Experiment with painting, crafting, writing, or music. These creative outlets can be both soothing and exhilarating.

By incorporating variety and excitement into your daily life in retirement, you transform each day into an opportunity for discovery and joy. Embrace the freedom to explore new experiences and cultivate a sense of wonder as you savor the rich tapestry of life in this remarkable chapter.

Chapter 4:
Travel Adventures

- **Discussing the benefits of travel in retirement**

Traveling in retirement is more than just sightseeing; it's a transformative experience that offers a multitude of physical, mental, and emotional benefits. Here are some compelling reasons why retirement is the perfect time to embark on exciting journeys:

1. Enriching Life Experiences:

Travel broadens horizons and exposes you to different cultures, traditions, and perspectives. It's a chance to gain a deeper understanding of the world, fostering personal growth and enriching your life experiences.

2. Physical Well-Being:

Exploring new destinations often involves physical activities like hiking, walking, or swimming. Travel keeps you active, contributing to improved fitness and overall health. It's an enjoyable way to stay physically engaged in retirement.

3. Mental Stimulation:

Travel challenges your mind. Learning about unfamiliar places, navigating new environments, and adapting to different cultures stimulate cognitive function. It can boost memory, problem-solving skills, and creativity.

4. Social Connections:

Travel provides opportunities to forge new friendships and strengthen existing relationships. Shared adventures create lasting bonds, and meeting people from diverse backgrounds enhances your social network.

5. Reduced Stress and Relaxation:

Taking a break from daily routines and responsibilities can significantly reduce stress levels. Relaxing in a new environment, whether it's a beachfront resort or a serene mountain retreat, rejuvenates your mind and body.

6. Cultural Immersion:

Travel allows you to immerse yourself in different cultures, taste exotic cuisines, and witness local customs. These experiences can foster a sense of cultural appreciation and empathy.

7. Sense of Adventure:

Retirement is the ideal time to embrace your adventurous spirit. Whether it's conquering a new hiking trail, embarking on a road trip, or taking a cruise to a far-flung destination, travel offers a sense of excitement and novelty.

8. Enhanced Creativity:

Exposure to diverse landscapes, art, and cultures can fuel your creativity. Travel often inspires new ideas, hobbies, or artistic pursuits that you may not have explored otherwise.

9. Time for Reflection:

Travel provides moments of solitude and reflection. Whether it's watching a sunset over the ocean or contemplating the grandeur of a historical site, it's an opportunity to reconnect with yourself and your aspirations.

10. Creating Lifelong Memories:

Travel memories are some of the most cherished and enduring. The stories, photos, and experiences from your journeys become a part of your personal narrative, something to share with loved ones and treasure for years to come.

11. Sense of Freedom:

In retirement, you have the freedom to travel without the constraints of work schedules or limited vacation time. It's a time to explore at your own pace and on your terms.

12. Fulfilling Bucket List Dreams:

Retirement often provides the opportunity to check off items from your bucket list. Whether it's visiting iconic landmarks, witnessing natural wonders, or pursuing specific travel goals, retirement is the time to make those dreams a reality.

Travel in retirement offers more than just leisure; it's an investment in your well-being and personal growth. It's a chance to explore, connect, and create lasting memories, making retirement a truly remarkable chapter in your life.

- **Overcoming travel challenges and concerns**

While travel in retirement can be incredibly rewarding, it's essential to address potential challenges and concerns to ensure a smooth and enjoyable experience. Here are some strategies for overcoming common travel-related issues:

1. Health and Wellness:

- **Consult with Your Healthcare Provider:** Before embarking on a journey, schedule a thorough check-up with your healthcare provider. Discuss any existing health conditions, vaccinations, and necessary medications.
- **Travel Insurance:** Invest in comprehensive travel insurance that covers medical emergencies, trip cancellations, and interruptions. Ensure the policy is tailored to your specific needs.

2. Mobility and Comfort:

- **Plan Ahead:** Research the accessibility of your chosen destination. If you have mobility concerns, ensure that accommodations, attractions, and transportation options are suitable for your needs.

- **Packing Wisely:** Pack comfortable shoes, clothing, and any mobility aids you may require. Don't forget to bring any necessary prescription medications and copies of medical records.

3. Safety and Security:

    - **Research Destination Safety:** Stay informed about the safety situation in your chosen destination. Check travel advisories and government websites for updates on safety concerns.
    - **Travel Documents:** Keep essential travel documents such as passports, visas, and travel insurance information in a secure, easily accessible location.

4. Financial Planning:

    - **Budgeting:** Create a realistic travel budget that accounts for all expenses, including accommodations, meals, transportation, and activities. Consider setting aside a contingency fund for unexpected costs.
    - **Currency Exchange:** Familiarize yourself with the local currency and exchange rates to avoid overpaying for goods and services. Use reputable exchange services or ATMs.

5. Language and Communication:

    - **Language Apps:** Download language translation apps or dictionaries to your smartphone. Learning a few basic phrases in the local language can be helpful and appreciated.
    - **Emergency Numbers:** Note down emergency contact numbers, including local authorities and your country's embassy or consulate in the destination.

6. Travel Companions:

    - **Traveling Solo:** If you're considering solo travel, research solo-friendly destinations and accommodations. Join travel groups or forums to connect with like-minded individuals.
    - **Choosing Companions:** If traveling with others, discuss expectations and preferences beforehand to ensure a harmonious travel experience.

7. Cultural Sensitivity:

    - **Research Cultural Norms:** Study the cultural norms and customs of your destination to show respect and avoid unintentional cultural misunderstandings.
    - **Dress Appropriately:** Dress modestly when visiting places of worship or conservative regions. Familiarize yourself with any dress codes or etiquette guidelines.

8. Travel Itinerary:

- **Flexibility:** While it's essential to have an itinerary, allow room for spontaneity and downtime. Overloading your schedule can lead to exhaustion and stress.
- **Local Insights:** Seek recommendations from locals or fellow travelers for off-the-beaten-path experiences and hidden gems.

9. Stay Informed:

- **Stay Updated:** Keep abreast of local news and developments, especially if you plan to visit remote or politically unstable areas. Adjust your plans if necessary.
- **Communication:** Stay connected with family and friends back home. Share your itinerary and contact details in case of emergencies.

By addressing these travel challenges and concerns proactively, you can minimize risks and maximize the enjoyment of your travels during retirement. With careful planning and consideration, your adventures can be both enriching and stress-free.

- **Listing exciting travel destinations**

Here are some exciting travel destinations to consider in retirement, each offering unique experiences and opportunities for exploration:

1. **Machu Picchu, Peru:** Explore the ancient Incan citadel nestled high in the Andes Mountains. Hike the Inca Trail or take a train to witness this archaeological wonder.
2. **Santorini, Greece:** Experience the stunning sunsets, white-washed buildings, and crystal-clear waters of this picturesque island in the Aegean Sea.
3. **Kyoto, Japan:** Immerse yourself in the rich culture, history, and beauty of Kyoto. Visit historic temples, gardens, and savor traditional Japanese cuisine.
4. **Banff National Park, Canada:** Discover the breathtaking landscapes of the Canadian Rockies. Hike, ski, or take a scenic drive through this natural wonderland.
5. **Tuscany, Italy:** Explore the rolling hills, vineyards, and charming villages of Tuscany. Enjoy fine wines, delicious cuisine, and artistic heritage.
6. **Bora Bora, French Polynesia:** Experience the epitome of tropical paradise with overwater bungalows, crystal-clear lagoons, and vibrant marine life.
7. **Iceland:** Witness the otherworldly beauty of Iceland, with its geothermal wonders, glaciers, waterfalls, and the Northern Lights.
8. **Barcelona, Spain:** Discover the unique architecture of Antoni Gaudí, indulge in tapas, and soak in the vibrant culture of this coastal city.

9. **African Safari:** Embark on a safari adventure in countries like Kenya, Tanzania, or South Africa to witness the incredible wildlife and landscapes.
10. **New Zealand:** Explore the diverse landscapes of New Zealand, from the fjords of Milford Sound to the geothermal wonders of Rotorua.
11. **Galápagos Islands, Ecuador:** Witness the incredible biodiversity and unique wildlife of this remote archipelago, which inspired Charles Darwin's theory of evolution.
12. **Amalfi Coast, Italy:** Drive along the scenic Amalfi Coast, with its dramatic cliffs, charming coastal towns, and exquisite Mediterranean views.
13. **Costa Rica:** Experience the lush rainforests, diverse wildlife, and adventure activities like zip-lining and hiking in this eco-friendly paradise.
14. **Prague, Czech Republic:** Wander through the fairy-tale-like streets of Prague, with its historic architecture, charming squares, and vibrant arts scene.
15. **Great Barrier Reef, Australia:** Dive or snorkel in the world's largest coral reef system, home to a stunning array of marine life and vibrant coral formations.
16. **Cape Town, South Africa:** Visit the iconic Table Mountain, explore the Cape Winelands, and discover the cultural diversity of this vibrant city.
17. **Patagonia, Chile and Argentina:** Trek through the pristine wilderness of Patagonia, known for its dramatic landscapes, glaciers, and rugged beauty.
18. **Bali, Indonesia:** Relax on idyllic beaches, explore ancient temples, and immerse yourself in Balinese culture and spirituality.
19. **Alaska, USA:** Cruise along the Inside Passage, witness glaciers, and encounter wildlife in one of the last great frontiers.
20. **Dubai, United Arab Emirates:** Experience the opulence and modernity of Dubai with its towering skyscrapers, luxury shopping, and desert adventures.

These are just a few of the countless exciting travel destinations around the world. Your choice of destination can be tailored to your interests, whether you're seeking adventure, relaxation, culture, or natural beauty.

- **Tips and resources for planning trips**

Planning trips in retirement can be a rewarding endeavor. Here are some tips and resources to help you plan your travels effectively:

Tips for Planning Trips:

1. **Set Clear Goals:** Determine the purpose and goals of your trip. Are you seeking relaxation, adventure, cultural experiences, or a mix of everything? Knowing your objectives will guide your planning.

2. **Create a Budget:** Establish a realistic travel budget that covers transportation, accommodation, meals, activities, and incidentals. Factor in a buffer for unexpected expenses.
3. **Research Destinations:** Explore travel websites, guidebooks, and blogs to research potential destinations. Consider factors like weather, safety, visa requirements, and local customs.
4. **Plan Ahead:** Start planning well in advance to secure the best deals on flights, accommodations, and tours. Many travel discounts are available for early bookings.
5. **Use Travel Apps:** Download travel apps for flight and hotel bookings, itinerary management, language translation, navigation, and local recommendations.
6. **Travel Insurance:** Invest in comprehensive travel insurance that covers health emergencies, trip cancellations, lost luggage, and other unforeseen events.
7. **Itinerary Planning:** Create a rough itinerary with a balance of activities and relaxation. Be flexible and leave room for spontaneous discoveries.
8. **Packing Smartly:** Pack lightly and efficiently. Consider the climate and activities at your destination. Don't forget essential items like passports, chargers, and travel adapters.
9. **Stay Organized:** Use travel organizers or apps to keep track of bookings, reservations, important documents, and travel-related information.
10. **Travel Documentation:** Ensure you have all required travel documents, including passports, visas, vaccination records, and a copy of your travel insurance policy.

Resources for Planning Trips:

1. **Travel Websites:** Websites like TripAdvisor, Expedia, Booking.com, and Airbnb provide information on accommodations, reviews, and bookings.
2. **Guidebooks:** Guidebooks from reputable publishers like Lonely Planet, Fodor's, and Rick Steves offer in-depth insights into destinations, accommodations, and activities.
3. **Travel Forums:** Participate in travel forums such as TripAdvisor's forums or Reddit's travel subreddits to seek advice, ask questions, and connect with experienced travelers.
4. **Travel Agencies:** Consider working with a travel agency, especially if you prefer personalized itineraries and expert advice. They can handle all aspects of your trip.
5. **Local Tourism Boards:** Visit the official websites of tourism boards for your chosen destination. They often provide valuable information, maps, and local insights.
6. **Travel Apps:** Download travel apps like Google Maps, TripAdvisor, Duolingo (for language learning), and currency converter apps to assist during your trip.
7. **Online Booking Platforms:** Use online booking platforms to find the best deals on flights (Skyscanner, Kayak), accommodations (Booking.com, Airbnb), and activities (Viator, GetYourGuide).
8. **Travel Insurance Providers:** Research and compare travel insurance providers to find coverage that suits your needs. Common providers include Allianz, World Nomads, and TravelGuard.

9. **Weather and Climate Apps:** Use weather apps like Weather.com or AccuWeather to check the climate and conditions at your destination during your planned travel dates.
10. **Government Resources:** Visit your country's government website for travel advisories, visa requirements, and safety information related to your destination.
11. **Travel Blogs and YouTube Channels:** Seek inspiration and practical advice from travel blogs and YouTube channels dedicated to specific destinations or travel experiences.

Remember that planning your trip is part of the adventure. Enjoy the process of researching, making arrangements, and looking forward to the exciting experiences that await you during your retirement travels.

Chapter 5
Home Sweet Home

- **Transforming your living space into a haven**

Transforming your living space into a haven in retirement is a wonderful way to create a comfortable and inviting environment for relaxation and enjoyment. Here are some tips to help you achieve this:

1. Declutter and Simplify:

- Start by decluttering your living space. Get rid of items you no longer need or use. Simplify your possessions to create a clean and organized environment.

2. Personalize Your Space:

- Add personal touches to your home, such as family photos, artwork, or sentimental objects. These reminders of happy memories can make your space feel warm and welcoming.

3. Choose Soothing Colors:

- Select calming colors for your walls and decor. Soft blues, greens, and neutrals can create a tranquil atmosphere. Consider your personal preferences and what colors bring you comfort.

4. Comfortable Furniture:

- Invest in comfortable furniture that suits your needs. Whether it's a cozy reading chair, a plush sofa, or ergonomic seating, prioritize comfort and functionality.

5. Create Cozy Nooks:

- Design cozy corners or reading nooks with comfortable seating, good lighting, and a small table for books and beverages. These spaces encourage relaxation and reflection.

6. Natural Elements:

- Incorporate natural elements like indoor plants, wooden furniture, and stone accents to bring the outdoors inside. Nature-inspired decor can promote tranquility.

7. Adequate Lighting:

- Ensure your living space has ample lighting. Use a mix of ambient, task, and accent lighting to create a well-lit and inviting atmosphere.

8. Organized Storage:

- Invest in storage solutions that keep your space clutter-free. Consider built-in shelving, storage ottomans, or wall-mounted storage units to maximize space.

9. Soundscapes and Music:

- Use soothing sounds or music to create a calming ambiance. Play your favorite tunes or explore nature sounds, meditation music, or ambient noise apps.

10. Cozy Textiles: Incorporate soft and cozy textiles like throws, cushions, and rugs. These not only add warmth but also enhance the comfort of your living space.

11. Aromatherapy: Use essential oils and diffusers to infuse your home with relaxing scents. Lavender, chamomile, and eucalyptus are popular choices for promoting calmness.

12. Art and Creativity: Express your creativity through art, crafts, or DIY projects. Display your creations or artworks that resonate with you, adding a personal touch to your space.

13. Minimal Electronics: Consider limiting the presence of electronic devices in your living space to reduce distractions and promote a sense of serenity.

14. Functional Layout: Arrange furniture in a way that optimizes the flow of your living space. Ensure that it's easy to move around and that each area serves its intended purpose.

15. Regular Maintenance: Maintain your living space by cleaning and organizing regularly. A well-maintained environment contributes to a sense of calm and well-being.

Creating a haven in your living space is a thoughtful and enjoyable project that can significantly enhance your retirement experience. Tailor your space to reflect your personality and preferences, and don't hesitate to make changes as your needs evolve. Ultimately, your home should be a place where you can find solace, relaxation, and joy during this special phase of life.

- **Decluttering and embracing minimalism**

Decluttering and embracing minimalism in retirement can be a liberating and refreshing experience. It allows you to simplify your life, reduce stress, and focus on the things that truly matter. Here are steps to help you declutter and embrace minimalism:

1. Set Clear Goals:

- Define your goals for decluttering and minimalism. Consider what you want to achieve, whether it's creating a more peaceful living space, reducing stress, or simplifying your daily life.

2. Start Small:

- Begin with a small and manageable area of your home, such as a single room or even a single drawer. This helps prevent overwhelm and builds confidence.

3. Sort and Categorize:

- Divide your possessions into categories such as clothes, books, kitchen items, and sentimental items. This step helps you see the scope of your belongings.

4. The KonMari Method:

- Consider using Marie Kondo's KonMari method, which involves evaluating each item based on whether it "sparks joy." Keep only the items that bring you joy and let go of the rest.

5. Declutter Gradually:

- Set aside time each day or week for decluttering. Slow and steady progress is often more sustainable and less stressful than attempting to declutter everything at once.

6. Donate and Recycle:

- Donate items in good condition to charitable organizations or pass them on to friends and family. Recycle or responsibly dispose of items that can't be reused.

7. Digital Declutter:

- Extend decluttering to your digital life. Delete unnecessary files, emails, and apps from your devices. Organize your digital documents and photos.

8. Minimalist Design:

- Embrace minimalist design principles in your home decor. Choose clean lines, neutral colors, and furniture with a purpose. Keep only meaningful decor items.

9. Quality Over Quantity:

- Focus on quality rather than quantity. Invest in well-made, durable items that serve their purpose effectively. Avoid accumulating multiples of the same thing.

10. Mindful Shopping:

- Practice mindful shopping by considering your purchases carefully. Ask yourself whether a new item adds value to your life or if it's just contributing to clutter.

11. Letting Go of Sentimentality:

- It can be challenging to part with sentimental items. Take photos or create digital records of these items to preserve memories while reducing physical clutter.

12. Embrace Empty Spaces:

- Don't be afraid of empty spaces in your home. Minimalism celebrates simplicity and the beauty of uncluttered areas.

13. Evaluate Your Commitments:

- Minimalism isn't limited to physical possessions. Consider decluttering your commitments and obligations. Prioritize activities and relationships that align with your values.

14. Reflect and Adjust:

- Periodically reflect on your progress and adjust your approach as needed. Minimalism is a journey, and your needs and preferences may change over time.

15. Enjoy the Benefits:

- Embrace the sense of freedom, clarity, and peace that comes with minimalism. Use your newfound time and space to focus on hobbies, relationships, and experiences that bring you joy.

Decluttering and embracing minimalism in retirement can lead to a more fulfilling and intentional way of living. It allows you to create a space that supports your well-being and helps you savor the simplicity and beauty of life in this phase.

- **Exploring hobbies and activities you can enjoy at home**

Exploring hobbies and activities you can enjoy at home is a wonderful way to make the most of your retirement and create a fulfilling daily routine. Here are some hobbies and activities to consider:

1. Reading:

- Dive into a good book, explore different genres, or join a book club to discuss your favorite reads with others.

2. Cooking and Baking:

- Experiment with new recipes, try your hand at gourmet cooking, or bake delicious treats for yourself and loved ones.

3. Gardening:

- Create a garden in your backyard or on your balcony. Cultivate flowers, herbs, vegetables, or even a small indoor garden.

4. Painting or Drawing:

- Tap into your creative side by taking up painting, drawing, or other forms of visual art. You don't need to be an expert to enjoy the process.

5. Music:

- Learn to play a musical instrument, sing, or simply enjoy listening to music. Music can be a great source of relaxation and creativity.

6. Writing:

- Start a journal, write poetry, short stories, or even a memoir. Writing can be a therapeutic and creative outlet.

7. Yoga and Meditation:

- Practice yoga or meditation to promote physical and mental well-being. You can follow online classes or use apps for guidance.

8. Photography:

- Explore the world of photography, whether it's capturing everyday moments, wildlife, or landscapes. Experiment with different techniques.

9. DIY Projects:

- Tackle DIY home improvement projects, craft projects, or woodworking. These activities can be both creative and practical.

10. Home Fitness:

- Stay active with home workouts, whether it's yoga, Pilates, strength training, or dance. Many fitness routines are available online.

11. Puzzles and Board Games:

- Challenge your mind with puzzles like crosswords, Sudoku, or jigsaw puzzles. Enjoy board games or card games with family and friends.

12. Learning:

- Take online courses or engage in lifelong learning. Explore subjects you're passionate about or pick up a new skill or language.

13. Home Decor and Design:

- Redecorate or renovate your living space. Experiment with interior design, rearrange furniture, or embark on DIY decor projects.

14. Birdwatching:

- Set up a bird feeder and enjoy birdwatching from your window or garden. Identify local bird species and learn about their habits.

15. Astronomy:

- Explore the night sky by taking up astronomy as a hobby. Invest in a telescope and study celestial objects and constellations.

16. Volunteering:

- Look for remote or virtual volunteer opportunities. You can contribute your skills and time to causes you're passionate about.

17. Film and TV:

- Watch classic films, explore new TV series, or even try your hand at filmmaking or video editing.

18. Online Gaming:

- Play video games, online puzzles, or engage in multiplayer online games to connect with others.

19. Collecting:

- Start a collection of items that interest you, such as coins, stamps, vintage items, or memorabilia.

20. Mindfulness and Relaxation:

- Practice mindfulness, relaxation techniques, or meditation to reduce stress and promote mental well-being.

Remember that retirement is a time to explore your interests and passions. Feel free to mix and match activities to create a well-rounded and enjoyable routine that suits your lifestyle and preferences.

Chapter 6
Embracing the Great Outdoors

- **Benefits of outdoor activities for physical health**

Engaging in outdoor activities offers a multitude of benefits for physical health. Here are some of the advantages:

1. Cardiovascular Health:

- Outdoor activities like hiking, cycling, jogging, or even brisk walking can significantly improve cardiovascular health. These activities increase heart rate and improve circulation, reducing the risk of heart disease.

2. Improved Fitness Levels:

- Regular outdoor activities help improve fitness levels by strengthening muscles, increasing endurance, and enhancing overall physical performance.

3. Weight Management:

- Outdoor activities help burn calories, making them an effective way to manage weight. Activities like hiking and swimming can burn a substantial number of calories.

4. Vitamin D Production:

- Exposure to natural sunlight allows the body to produce vitamin D, which is crucial for bone health, immune function, and overall well-being.

5. Stronger Immune System:

- Spending time outdoors and engaging in physical activity can boost the immune system. Fresh air, exposure to nature, and increased physical activity contribute to a healthier immune response.

6. Stress Reduction:

- Outdoor activities promote relaxation and reduce stress levels. Spending time in natural settings, known as "forest bathing" or "shinrin-yoku," has been shown to lower cortisol levels and improve mood.

7. Enhanced Mental Health:

- Outdoor physical activity can improve mental health by reducing symptoms of anxiety and depression. The combination of exercise and exposure to nature has a positive impact on mood and overall well-being.

8. Better Sleep Quality:

- Regular outdoor activities can help regulate sleep patterns and improve sleep quality. Exposure to natural light during the day can also help with maintaining a healthy circadian rhythm.

9. Balance and Coordination:

- Outdoor activities often involve navigating uneven terrain, which can improve balance and coordination over time. This is especially beneficial as we age.

10. Social Interaction:

- Many outdoor activities are group-oriented, providing opportunities for social interaction and building relationships. Strong social connections are linked to better overall health.

11. Stress Reduction:

- Spending time in natural outdoor settings can reduce stress and anxiety. The sights and sounds of nature have a calming effect on the mind and body.

12. Increased Vitamin Intake:

- Outdoor activities such as gardening can provide opportunities to grow your own fruits and vegetables, increasing your intake of vitamins and minerals.

13. Enhanced Respiratory Health:

- Outdoor activities can lead to deeper breathing and improved lung function, particularly in areas with fresh, clean air.

14. Better Bone Health: Activities like hiking and walking can help improve bone density and reduce the risk of osteoporosis, especially when combined with exposure to vitamin D from sunlight.

15. Reduced Sedentary Time:

- Outdoor activities encourage people to spend less time sitting and more time moving, which reduces the negative health effects associated with prolonged sedentary behavior.

Overall, outdoor activities offer a holistic approach to physical health, combining exercise, exposure to nature, social interaction, and stress reduction to promote a healthier and more active lifestyle. Incorporating outdoor activities into your routine can have a positive and lasting impact on your physical well-being.

- **Incorporating outdoor exercise into your routine**

Incorporating outdoor exercise into your routine is a great way to stay active, improve physical fitness, and enjoy the benefits of spending time in nature. Here are some tips to help you get started:

1. Choose Activities You Enjoy:

- The key to sticking with outdoor exercise is selecting activities you genuinely enjoy. Whether it's hiking, cycling, jogging, swimming, or playing a sport, find something that makes you look forward to being active outdoors.

2. Set Realistic Goals:

- Start with achievable goals, such as going for a 30-minute walk three times a week or completing a beginner's hiking trail. Gradually increase the intensity and duration of your outdoor workouts as your fitness level improves.

3. Create a Schedule:

- Establish a regular exercise schedule that suits your lifestyle. Consistency is key to reaping the benefits of outdoor exercise.

4. Find Exercise Partners:

- Invite friends, family members, or neighbors to join you for outdoor workouts. Having exercise partners can provide motivation and make the experience more enjoyable.

5. Explore Different Locations:

- Keep things interesting by exploring various outdoor settings. Visit local parks, nature reserves, beaches, or trails to add variety to your workouts.

6. Warm-Up and Cool Down:

- Prior to any outdoor exercise, perform a proper warm-up to prepare your muscles and joints. After your workout, cool down with gentle stretching to prevent soreness.

7. Dress Appropriately:

- Wear comfortable and weather-appropriate clothing. Dress in layers for cooler weather, and don't forget sunscreen, a hat, and sunglasses for sun protection.

8. Stay Hydrated:

- Bring a reusable water bottle to stay hydrated during your outdoor workouts, especially in warm weather.

9. Safety First:

- Ensure your safety by following traffic rules when cycling or jogging on roads. If you're hiking in remote areas, inform someone of your plans and bring necessary supplies.

10. Use Technology:

- Consider using fitness apps or wearable devices to track your progress and set goals. Many apps provide guided workouts and GPS tracking for outdoor activities.

11. Mix It Up:

- Keep your outdoor workouts diverse by incorporating different exercises. For example, combine walking with bodyweight exercises like push-ups, squats, and lunges.

12. Practice Mindfulness:

- Use your outdoor exercise time as an opportunity to practice mindfulness and connect with nature. Pay attention to the sights, sounds, and sensations around you.

13. Consider Classes or Groups:

- Join outdoor fitness classes or groups in your community. Yoga in the park, group hikes, or outdoor boot camps can add a social element to your workouts.

14. Be Patient and Listen to Your Body:

- It's essential to listen to your body and avoid pushing yourself too hard. Gradual progress is key to preventing injuries and enjoying sustainable fitness gains.

15. Reward Yourself:

- After a successful outdoor workout, reward yourself with something you enjoy, whether it's a healthy snack, a soothing shower, or a moment of relaxation in nature.

Incorporating outdoor exercise into your routine not only benefits your physical health but also enhances your mental and emotional well-being. It provides an opportunity to connect with the natural world, reduce stress, and boost your overall quality of life in retirement.

- **Birdwatching, hiking, and other nature-focused activities**

Engaging in nature-focused activities like birdwatching and hiking can be incredibly rewarding during retirement. These activities not only promote physical health but also provide a sense of tranquility and connection with the natural world. Here's a closer look at birdwatching, hiking, and other nature-focused pursuits:

1. Birdwatching:

- Birdwatching involves observing and identifying birds in their natural habitats. It's a peaceful and meditative activity that requires minimal equipment, making it accessible to people of all ages.

Benefits:

- Enhances mindfulness and patience.
- Encourages outdoor exploration.
- Fosters an appreciation for wildlife.
- Can be enjoyed individually or in groups.
- Promotes learning about local ecosystems and bird species.

2. Hiking:

- Hiking allows you to explore natural landscapes on foot. It can range from leisurely walks on well-maintained trails to challenging hikes in remote wilderness areas.

Benefits:

- Improves cardiovascular fitness and strength.
- Connects you with nature and reduces stress.
- Provides opportunities for social interaction when hiking with others.
- Allows for exploration of diverse terrains and ecosystems.
- Offers a sense of accomplishment and adventure.

3. Gardening:

- Gardening involves tending to plants, flowers, and vegetables in your own outdoor space. It's a creative and fulfilling way to connect with nature and nurture living things.

Benefits:

- Provides physical activity and gentle exercise.
- Enhances mental well-being and reduces stress.
- Allows you to grow your own produce and herbs.
- Creates a beautiful and personalized outdoor space.
- Offers a sense of purpose and accomplishment.

4. Nature Photography:

- Nature photography combines the love of the outdoors with artistic expression. Capture the beauty of landscapes, wildlife, and natural phenomena through your lens.

Benefits:

- Encourages mindfulness and attention to detail.
- Fosters creativity and artistic growth.
- Allows you to share your perspective of the natural world.
- Provides opportunities for exploration and travel.
- Creates lasting memories and visual records of your experiences.

5. Camping:

- Camping involves spending time outdoors, often in remote or natural settings, where you can connect with nature, explore, and enjoy activities like hiking, fishing, and stargazing.

Benefits:

- Provides a break from daily routines and technology.
- Offers a sense of adventure and self-reliance.
- Encourages physical activity and outdoor skills.
- Promotes relaxation and quality time with loved ones.
- Allows you to immerse yourself in natural environments.

6. Nature Conservation and Volunteering:

- Get involved in conservation efforts by volunteering with local environmental organizations. Participate in clean-up initiatives, tree planting, or habitat restoration projects.

Benefits:

- Fosters a sense of purpose and contribution.
- Connects you with like-minded individuals and communities.
- Supports the preservation of natural resources.
- Provides opportunities to learn about ecosystems and conservation practices.
- Encourages outdoor teamwork and cooperation.

Whether you're an avid birder, a passionate hiker, or someone looking to reconnect with nature in retirement, these activities offer numerous physical, mental, and emotional benefits. They provide opportunities to explore the great outdoors, learn about the natural world, and cultivate a deeper appreciation for the environment and all its wonders.

- **Finding solace and joy in the natural world**

Finding solace and joy in the natural world is a profound and deeply fulfilling experience. Nature has a unique way of nurturing our physical, mental, and emotional well-being. Here are some ways to connect with and find solace and joy in the natural world during retirement:

1. Spend Time Outdoors: Make it a habit to spend regular time outdoors, whether it's in your garden, a local park, or a nearby natural reserve. Nature's beauty and tranquility can have a calming and rejuvenating effect.

2. Practice Mindfulness: Embrace mindfulness by immersing yourself fully in the natural environment. Pay attention to the sights, sounds, and sensations around you. This can help reduce stress and increase your appreciation for the world around you.

3. Birdwatching: Birdwatching is a peaceful and meditative activity that allows you to observe and identify different bird species. It's a way to connect with nature and its diverse inhabitants.

4. Take Nature Walks: Go for leisurely nature walks or hikes. Explore local trails, forests, or coastal areas to discover the beauty of your surroundings and enjoy the benefits of physical activity.

5. Enjoy Sunrises and Sunsets: Witnessing a sunrise or sunset in a natural setting can be a breathtaking and soul-soothing experience. Plan outings to catch these magical moments.

6. Star Gazing: On clear nights, venture out to a dark area away from city lights and gaze at the stars. Astronomy can deepen your connection to the universe and instill a sense of wonder.

7. Nature Journaling: Keep a nature journal to record your observations, sketches, and reflections on your outdoor experiences. This practice can help you deepen your connection to the natural world.

8. Picnics and Outdoor Dining: Enjoy meals outdoors whenever possible. Whether it's a picnic in the park or dining on your patio, eating in nature adds a sense of pleasure to your culinary experiences.

9. Photography: Capture the beauty of the natural world through photography. Document the changing seasons, landscapes, and wildlife, allowing you to relive these moments later.

10. Listen to Nature's Sounds: Sit quietly and listen to the sounds of nature—birdsong, rustling leaves, flowing water, or the wind in the trees. These sounds can be incredibly soothing.

11. Engage in Outdoor Activities: Participate in outdoor activities you love, such as gardening, fishing, kayaking, or camping. These pursuits offer a sense of adventure and connection to the environment.

12. Volunteer for Conservation: Get involved in conservation efforts by volunteering with organizations dedicated to preserving natural habitats. Contributing to the protection of the natural world can be deeply fulfilling.

13. Share Nature with Loved Ones: Invite family and friends to join you in your outdoor adventures. Sharing the joy of nature with others can enhance your own appreciation.

14. Disconnect from Technology: Consider unplugging from digital devices and screens during your outdoor excursions. Disconnecting allows you to fully immerse yourself in the natural world.

15. Reflect and Meditate: Find a quiet spot in nature to reflect, meditate, or practice yoga. These activities can foster inner peace and a sense of harmony with the environment.

The natural world offers solace, joy, and a deep sense of connection to something greater than ourselves. It provides an opportunity to slow down, appreciate the beauty of life, and find inner peace during retirement.

Chapter 7
Fitness for Life

- **Discussing the significance of staying physically active**

Staying physically active is of paramount significance throughout life, and it takes on even greater importance during retirement. Here are some key reasons why staying physically active is crucial in retirement:

1. Overall Health and Well-Being:

- Physical activity is essential for maintaining good health and well-being. Regular exercise helps prevent chronic diseases such as heart disease, diabetes, hypertension, and osteoporosis.

2. Weight Management:

- Physical activity helps control body weight by burning calories. Maintaining a healthy weight reduces the risk of obesity-related health issues.

3. Cardiovascular Health:

- Exercise strengthens the heart and improves cardiovascular health. It reduces the risk of heart disease, lowers blood pressure, and enhances circulation.

4. Bone Health:

- Weight-bearing exercises, such as walking, jogging, and weightlifting, help maintain bone density and reduce the risk of osteoporosis and fractures.

5. Muscle Strength and Function:

- Regular physical activity preserves muscle mass and strength, which is crucial for maintaining mobility and independence as you age.

6. Joint Health:

- Exercise can help lubricate and protect the joints. It can also improve joint flexibility and reduce the risk of arthritis-related pain and stiffness.

7. Mental Health:

- Physical activity has a profound impact on mental health. It reduces symptoms of depression and anxiety, enhances mood, and boosts cognitive function.

8. Cognitive Health:

- Staying physically active is linked to improved cognitive function and a reduced risk of cognitive decline and dementia in older adults.

9. Balance and Fall Prevention:

- Balance exercises and strength training can help prevent falls, a common concern in older age. This reduces the risk of serious injuries.

10. Social Interaction:

- Participating in group physical activities, such as sports, classes, or walking groups, provides social interaction and fosters a sense of belonging.

11. Quality of Life:

- Staying active enhances overall quality of life. It increases energy levels, helps with daily tasks, and allows for more active participation in hobbies and interests.

12. Stress Reduction:

- Exercise is an excellent stress reliever. Physical activity triggers the release of endorphins, which promote feelings of happiness and reduce stress.

13. Increased Longevity:

- Numerous studies have shown that regular physical activity is associated with a longer lifespan. It can add years to your life and life to your years.

14. Maintaining Independence:

- Being physically active enables you to maintain your independence as you age. It helps you perform daily activities without assistance for a longer period.

15. Enjoyment and Fulfillment:

- Engaging in physical activities you enjoy can bring a sense of fulfillment and joy to your retirement years. It provides opportunities for adventure and new experiences.

The significance of staying physically active in retirement cannot be overstated. It not only contributes to a longer and healthier life but also enhances the quality of that life. The key is to find physical activities you enjoy and make them a regular part of your daily or weekly routine. Whether it's walking, dancing, swimming, or playing a sport, staying active is an investment in your physical, mental, and emotional well-being.

16. Enhanced Sleep: Regular physical activity can lead to better sleep patterns and improved sleep quality. Quality sleep is essential for overall health and well-being.

17. Stress Management: Exercise is a natural stress reliever. Engaging in physical activity helps reduce cortisol levels and promotes relaxation.

18. Immune System Boost: Staying active can bolster your immune system, making your body better equipped to fight off illnesses and infections.

19. Social Connection: Participating in group activities and fitness classes can expand your social circle and provide opportunities to forge new friendships during retirement.

20. Weight-Bearing Exercise: Weight-bearing exercises, like walking or dancing, help maintain bone density, reducing the risk of fractures and osteoporosis.

21. Heart Health: Regular exercise supports heart health by improving circulation, reducing inflammation, and lowering the risk of heart disease.

22. Pain Management: Physical activity can help alleviate chronic pain conditions, such as arthritis, by increasing joint flexibility and reducing inflammation.

23. Confidence and Self-Esteem: Staying physically active can boost your self-confidence and self-esteem as you achieve fitness milestones and feel better about your body.

24. Brain Health: Physical activity has been linked to improved cognitive function and memory. It can help keep your mind sharp in retirement.

25. Lifelong Learning: Staying active encourages an ongoing interest in learning about fitness, nutrition, and health, fostering a growth mindset.

26. Inspiration for Others: Leading an active and healthy lifestyle in retirement can inspire friends and family members to do the same, promoting a culture of well-being.

27. Sense of Achievement: Setting and achieving fitness goals, whether big or small, provides a sense of accomplishment and motivation to keep pushing yourself.

28. Independence: Maintaining physical fitness allows you to maintain your independence for longer, reducing the need for assistance with daily activities.

29. Nature Connection: Engaging in outdoor activities, such as hiking or gardening, enhances your connection with the natural world and encourages environmental stewardship.

30. Better Pain Tolerance: Regular exercise can increase pain tolerance, making it easier to cope with minor aches and discomforts that come with aging.

31. Improved Digestion: Physical activity can aid in digestion and alleviate digestive issues, leading to better overall gut health.

32. Creativity and Problem Solving: Exercise has been shown to enhance creativity and problem-solving skills, which can benefit various aspects of life in retirement.

33. Reduced Healthcare Costs: Staying active can lead to fewer health issues and lower healthcare costs in the long run, allowing you to enjoy retirement with fewer financial worries.

34. Positive Lifestyle Habits: Regular exercise often leads to other positive lifestyle habits, such as maintaining a balanced diet and avoiding harmful behaviors like smoking.

35. Lifelong Adventure: Staying active ensures that retirement is a continuous adventure, filled with opportunities to explore new activities and places.

36. Emotional Resilience: Exercise fosters emotional resilience, helping you better cope with life's challenges and setbacks.

37. Sense of Purpose: Maintaining an active lifestyle can provide a sense of purpose in retirement, giving you something to look forward to each day.

- **Different types of exercise and their benefits**

There are various types of exercise, each offering unique benefits for physical health, mental well-being, and overall fitness. Here are some common types of exercise and their respective advantages:

1. Cardiovascular Exercise (Aerobic Exercise):

- Benefits:
    - Improved heart and lung health.
    - Enhanced cardiovascular fitness.
    - Weight management and calorie burn.
    - Reduced risk of heart disease.
- **Examples:** Running, jogging, cycling, swimming, brisk walking, dancing, and aerobics.

2. Strength Training (Resistance Exercise):

- Benefits:
    - Increased muscle strength and endurance.
    - Enhanced metabolism and calorie burning.
    - Improved bone density and joint health.
    - Better functional fitness for daily tasks.
- **Examples:** Weight lifting, bodyweight exercises (push-ups, squats, lunges), resistance band workouts.

3. Flexibility and Stretching Exercises:

- Benefits:
    - Improved range of motion and joint flexibility.
    - Reduced risk of injuries and muscle soreness.
    - Enhanced posture and balance.
    - Stress reduction and relaxation.
- **Examples:** Yoga, Pilates, static stretching, dynamic stretching.

4. Balance and Stability Exercises:

- Benefits:
    - Better balance and coordination.
    - Reduced risk of falls and injuries, especially in older adults.
    - Improved core strength.
    - Enhanced functional fitness.
- **Examples:** Tai Chi, balance board exercises, stability ball workouts.

5. High-Intensity Interval Training (HIIT):

- Benefits:
    - Efficient and time-effective workouts.
    - Improved cardiovascular fitness.
    - Increased calorie burn and metabolism.
    - Muscle strengthening and endurance.
- **Examples:** Short bursts of intense exercises followed by brief rest periods (e.g., sprinting followed by walking).

6. Low-Impact Exercises:

- Benefits:
    - Reduced stress on joints.
    - Suitable for individuals with joint pain or injuries.
    - Cardiovascular fitness without high impact.
    - Enhanced endurance and muscle tone.
- **Examples:** Swimming, water aerobics, cycling, elliptical training.

7. Functional Fitness Exercises:

- Benefits:
    - Improved ability to perform everyday tasks.

- Enhanced muscle strength and flexibility.
- Reduced risk of injuries during daily activities.
- Better posture and body mechanics.
- **Examples:** Functional movements like squats, lunges, and planks.

8. Mind-Body Exercises:

- Benefits:
  - Stress reduction and relaxation.
  - Improved mental focus and mindfulness.
  - Enhanced mind-body connection.
  - Flexibility and physical fitness.
- **Examples:** Yoga, Tai Chi, Qigong, Pilates.

9. Outdoor Activities:

- Benefits:
  - Connection with nature and mental well-being.
  - Improved cardiovascular fitness.
  - Fresh air and vitamin D from sunlight.
  - Opportunity for adventure and exploration.
- **Examples:** Hiking, birdwatching, gardening, cycling, kayaking.

10. Group Exercise Classes:

- Benefits:
- Social interaction and community.
- Motivation and accountability.
- Structured and guided workouts.
- Variety in exercise routines.

Examples: Group fitness classes like Zumba, spinning, step aerobics, and group strength training.

11. Sports and Recreational Activities:

- Benefits:
- Enjoyment and engagement.
- Teamwork and competition (if desired).
- Improved physical fitness and skill development.
- Opportunities for social interaction.

Examples: Tennis, golf, soccer, basketball, swimming, and racquetball.

12. Mindful Movement Practices:

- Benefits:
- Stress reduction and relaxation.
- Enhanced body awareness and mindfulness.
- Improved posture and flexibility.
- A holistic approach to physical and mental well-being.

Examples: Feldenkrais Method, Alexander Technique, somatic movement.

Incorporating a combination of these exercise types into your routine can provide a well-rounded approach to physical fitness and overall health. Tailor your exercise regimen to your preferences, fitness goals, and any specific health considerations you may have. Remember that staying active is a lifelong journey, and variety can help keep your workouts enjoyable and effective.

- **Tailoring fitness activities to your interests**

Tailoring fitness activities to your interests is a key strategy for maintaining an active and enjoyable lifestyle in retirement. By choosing activities that you genuinely love, you are more likely to stay motivated and make exercise a consistent part of your daily routine. Here's how to customize your fitness activities to align with your interests:

1. Identify Your Passions:

- Start by identifying your hobbies and interests. What activities make you excited and bring you joy? Whether it's dancing, hiking, gardening, or something else, these passions can serve as the foundation for your fitness routine.

2. Explore New Interests:

- Retirement is an excellent time to explore new interests and hobbies that you may not have had time for in the past. Be open to trying new things and discovering activities that capture your imagination.

3. Combine Fitness with Fun:

- Look for ways to combine physical activity with your interests. For example, if you love nature, consider birdwatching hikes or photography outings. If you're a music enthusiast, dancing or playing a musical instrument can be great choices.

4. Join Clubs and Groups:

- Seek out clubs or groups that align with your interests and offer opportunities for physical activity. Joining a local hiking club, dance class, or gardening association can provide social support and motivation.

5. Set Goals and Challenges:

- Set specific fitness goals related to your interests. For example, if you enjoy hiking, aim to conquer a particular trail or reach a specific summit. Having goals can add excitement and purpose to your workouts.

6. Create a Dedicated Space:

- If your interests involve specific activities that require space, create a dedicated area at home. This could be a dance studio, gardening space, or a workshop for DIY projects.

7. Customize Your Routine:

- Tailor your fitness routine to match your interests. For instance, if you're a nature lover, incorporate outdoor workouts like hiking, cycling, or paddleboarding. If you're a book enthusiast, listen to audiobooks or podcasts while walking.

8. Embrace Seasonal Activities:

- Take advantage of seasonal interests. For example, enjoy skiing or snowshoeing in the winter and switch to gardening or outdoor yoga in the warmer months.

9. Seek Out Specialty Classes:

- Look for specialty fitness classes that align with your interests. These might include dance classes like salsa or tango, watercolor painting combined with yoga, or Tai Chi in a serene park setting.

10. Mix and Match:

- Don't limit yourself to just one activity. Mix and match different fitness activities that align with various interests. This keeps your routine fresh and engaging.

12. Involve Loved Ones:

- Encourage family members or friends to participate in your fitness activities. Sharing your interests with loved ones can create meaningful bonding experiences.

13. Track Progress and Celebrate Achievements:

- Keep a record of your fitness achievements related to your interests. Celebrate milestones and use them as motivation to continue pursuing your passions.

14. Adapt to Changing Interests:

- Interests can evolve over time. Be flexible and open to adapting your fitness activities to align with your changing passions and preferences.

15. Enjoy the Process:

- Above all, remember that fitness should be enjoyable. If an activity becomes a chore, consider trying something new or adjusting your approach to make it more fun.

By integrating your interests into your fitness routine, you can create a sustainable and fulfilling way to stay active in retirement. It's not only about staying fit but also about embracing the activities that bring joy and meaning to your life.

- **Making exercise an enjoyable part of your daily life**

Making exercise an enjoyable and sustainable part of your daily life is key to reaping its long-term benefits. Here are some strategies to help you embrace exercise as a regular and pleasurable activity:

1. Choose Activities You Love:

- Select exercises that genuinely interest and excite you. Whether it's dancing, hiking, swimming, or gardening, finding joy in the activity is essential.

2. Set Realistic Goals:

- Establish achievable fitness goals that align with your interests and abilities. Goals can provide motivation and a sense of accomplishment.

3. Create a Routine:

- Incorporate exercise into your daily schedule, just like any other appointment or commitment. Consistency is vital for making exercise a habit.

4. Find an Exercise Buddy:

- Partnering with a friend or family member can make workouts more enjoyable and provide accountability.

5. Try Group Classes:

- Group fitness classes offer a social aspect and a structured workout. Join classes that align with your interests, such as yoga, dance, or group cycling.

6. Listen to Music or Audiobooks:

- Create a workout playlist of your favorite songs or listen to audiobooks, podcasts, or motivational talks during your workouts to make the time pass quickly.

7. Vary Your Routine:

- Keep exercise exciting by varying your activities. Try new workouts, explore different locations, or change up your routine periodically.

8. Set the Right Atmosphere:

- Create a pleasant exercise environment. Play upbeat music, exercise in well-ventilated spaces, or take your workouts outdoors to enjoy nature.

9. Reward Yourself:

- Treat yourself with small rewards after completing a workout or achieving a fitness milestone. It could be a favorite healthy snack, a relaxing bath, or a guilt-free indulgence.

10. Track Your Progress:

- Use fitness apps or journals to track your progress. Seeing improvements can be motivating and reinforce your commitment to exercise.

11. Embrace Mindfulness:

- Be present during your workouts. Focus on how your body feels and the positive impact exercise has on your well-being. Mindfulness can enhance your enjoyment.

12. Mix Up Your Workouts:

- Incorporate a mix of cardio, strength training, flexibility, and balance exercises to keep your routine well-rounded and engaging.

13. Make It Social:

- Invite friends or family to join you in physical activities. Consider organizing group outings like hiking trips or sports games.

14. Compete in Fun Challenges:

- Participate in fitness challenges or events that align with your interests. It could be a charity walk, a local 5K run, or a dance competition.

15. Focus on the Benefits:

- Remind yourself of the numerous physical and mental benefits of exercise. This can reinforce your commitment to making it a regular part of your life.

16. Be Kind to Yourself:

- Don't be too hard on yourself if you miss a workout or face setbacks. Understand that it's normal, and the key is to get back on track without self-criticism.

17. Celebrate Small Wins:

- Celebrate the small victories along your fitness journey. Every step counts, and recognizing your progress can boost your motivation.

18. Seek Professional Guidance:

- Consider working with a personal trainer or fitness coach who can design a tailored workout plan that aligns with your interests and goals.

Making exercise enjoyable is essential for turning it into a lifelong habit. By finding activities you love, staying consistent, and focusing on the positive aspects of fitness, you can make exercise a natural and fulfilling part of your daily life in retirement.

Chapter 8
Nourishing the Soul

- **Exploring the importance of mental health in retirement**

Exploring the importance of mental health in retirement is crucial, as this life stage can bring both opportunities and challenges that significantly impact one's emotional well-being. Here's an overview of why mental health in retirement matters and how to prioritize it:

1. Transition and Adjustment: Retirement marks a significant life transition. For many, it involves shifting from a structured work environment to newfound freedom. This adjustment can lead to feelings of uncertainty, loss of identity, or a lack of purpose, making mental health support essential.

2. Identity and Purpose: Work often provides a sense of identity and purpose. In retirement, individuals may need to explore new sources of meaning and fulfillment to maintain a strong sense of self-worth.

3. Social Connections: The workplace often serves as a primary source of social interaction. In retirement, there may be a risk of social isolation, which can contribute to feelings of loneliness and depression. Maintaining and nurturing social connections is crucial for mental well-being.

4. Financial Concerns: Retirement can bring financial stressors, such as managing a fixed income, healthcare costs, and unexpected expenses. These concerns can impact mental health if not addressed proactively.

5. Health and Physical Well-Being: Aging-related health challenges can affect mental health. Chronic pain, illness, or cognitive decline can lead to anxiety and depression. Prioritizing physical health through exercise, nutrition, and regular healthcare check-ups is vital.

6. Time Management: Suddenly having ample free time in retirement can be a double-edged sword. While it provides opportunities for leisure and hobbies, it can also lead to boredom or a sense of unproductiveness. Learning effective time management and goal setting can help combat these issues.

7. Stress Management: Effective stress management techniques are essential in retirement, as stressors may shift but not necessarily decrease. Learning mindfulness, relaxation exercises, or seeking therapy can help manage stress effectively.

8. Mental Stimulation: Continuing to engage in intellectually stimulating activities is essential for cognitive health. Reading, learning new skills, puzzles, or pursuing creative hobbies can keep the mind sharp.

9. Self-Care: Prioritizing self-care is crucial. This includes getting enough sleep, eating a balanced diet, staying hydrated, and managing chronic conditions effectively.

10. Seeking Support: Recognizing the importance of seeking help when needed is a sign of strength. If you experience persistent feelings of sadness, anxiety, or hopelessness, consider talking to a mental health professional.

11. Volunteering and Giving Back: Engaging in volunteer work or community involvement can provide a sense of purpose and satisfaction in retirement. Giving back to others can boost mental well-being.

12. Emotional Resilience: Building emotional resilience is valuable in navigating the challenges of retirement. This involves developing coping strategies and a positive mindset to bounce back from setbacks.

13. Maintaining a Support System: Surrounding oneself with a supportive network of friends, family, and peers who understand the challenges of retirement can provide emotional support and a sense of belonging.

14. Setting Goals: Setting and working towards personal goals in retirement can offer structure and motivation. These goals can be related to hobbies, travel, education, or any area of personal interest.

15. Embracing New Experiences: Retirement is an opportunity to explore new interests, hobbies, and experiences. Embracing novelty can invigorate the mind and enhance mental well-being.

16. Mind-Body Connection: Recognizing the strong connection between physical and mental health is essential. Regular exercise, a balanced diet, and adequate sleep all contribute to better mental health outcomes.

17. Professional Guidance: Consulting with mental health professionals, such as therapists or counselors, can provide valuable tools and strategies for maintaining mental well-being in retirement.

In summary, mental health in retirement is a critical aspect of overall well-being. It requires proactive efforts to address the unique challenges and opportunities this life stage presents. By prioritizing mental health, seeking support when needed, and embracing the joys of retirement, individuals can enjoy this phase of life with greater contentment and fulfillment.

- **Mindfulness, meditation, and their benefits**

Mindfulness and meditation are practices that cultivate a heightened state of awareness, attention, and presence in the present moment. These practices offer numerous physical, mental, and emotional benefits, making them valuable tools for enhancing overall well-being. Here's an overview of mindfulness, meditation, and their benefits:

Mindfulness: Mindfulness is the practice of intentionally paying attention to the present moment without judgment. It involves being fully aware of your thoughts, feelings, sensations, and surroundings as they occur. Mindfulness can be practiced informally in daily life or through formal meditation techniques.

Meditation: Meditation is a structured practice that often involves focused attention, controlled breathing, and relaxation techniques. There are various forms of meditation, including mindfulness meditation, loving-kindness meditation, and transcendental meditation, among others.

Benefits of Mindfulness and Meditation:

1. Stress Reduction:

- Mindfulness and meditation are powerful tools for reducing stress. They activate the body's relaxation response, lower cortisol (stress hormone) levels, and promote a sense of calm.

2. Improved Emotional Regulation:

- These practices enhance emotional intelligence by helping individuals become more aware of their emotions, allowing them to respond to situations with greater emotional control.

3. Enhanced Concentration and Focus:

- Mindfulness and meditation improve attention span and concentration by training the mind to stay present and avoid distractions.

4. Anxiety and Depression Management:

- These practices can be effective in reducing symptoms of anxiety and depression. They help individuals break free from ruminative thought patterns and create a more positive mental state.

5. Pain Management:

- Mindfulness and meditation have been shown to reduce the perception of pain and improve pain tolerance, making them valuable in managing chronic pain conditions.

6. Better Sleep:

- Mindfulness and meditation can improve sleep quality by reducing racing thoughts and promoting relaxation, making it easier to fall asleep and stay asleep.

7. Increased Self-Awareness:

- These practices encourage self-reflection and self-discovery, leading to a deeper understanding of one's thoughts, behaviors, and motivations.

8. Greater Resilience:

- Regular practice of mindfulness and meditation can build emotional resilience, helping individuals bounce back more effectively from life's challenges.

9. Enhanced Relationships:

- By developing greater empathy and emotional regulation, these practices can improve communication and relationship dynamics.

10. Reduced Symptoms of Post-Traumatic Stress Disorder (PTSD): Mindfulness-based interventions have shown promise in reducing symptoms of PTSD by helping individuals process traumatic memories.

11. Lower Blood Pressure: Meditation has been linked to lower blood pressure, reducing the risk of hypertension and cardiovascular issues.

12. Immune System Support: Mindfulness and meditation can boost the immune system's functioning, helping the body better defend against illness.

13. Greater Overall Well-Being: By promoting a positive outlook, reducing stress, and improving emotional and physical health, mindfulness and meditation contribute to a sense of overall well-being.

14. Cognitive Benefits: These practices can enhance cognitive function, including memory, problem-solving, and creativity.

15. Increased Compassion and Empathy: Loving-kindness meditation, a specific form of meditation, fosters compassion and empathy towards oneself and others.

16. Personal Growth and Transformation: Mindfulness and meditation can lead to personal growth, self-acceptance, and a deeper sense of purpose and meaning in life.

To experience these benefits, it's essential to practice mindfulness and meditation regularly. You can start with short sessions and gradually increase the duration as you become more comfortable with the practice. Whether through guided meditations, classes, or self-guided practice, incorporating mindfulness and meditation into your daily routine can lead to profound positive changes in your life.

- **Practicing mindfulness in everyday activities**

Practicing mindfulness in everyday activities involves bringing your full attention and awareness to the present moment, no matter what you're doing. It's a way to cultivate mindfulness throughout your daily life and can help reduce stress, enhance focus, and promote overall well-being. Here are some tips for incorporating mindfulness into everyday activities:

1. Mindful Breathing:

- Start by taking a few deep breaths and centering yourself before beginning any activity. Pay attention to the sensation of your breath entering and leaving your body. This simple act can help you stay grounded and present.

2. Mindful Eating:

- When you eat, do so without distractions like TV or smartphones. Pay attention to the flavors, textures, and smells of your food. Chew slowly and savor each bite. Notice the sensation of hunger and fullness.

3. Mindful Walking:

- Whether you're walking indoors or outdoors, focus on the act of walking itself. Feel the ground beneath your feet, the movement of your legs, and the rhythm of your steps. Notice the sights and sounds around you without judgment.

4. Mindful Listening:

- When engaged in conversations or listening to music, truly listen. Put aside the urge to formulate responses and instead concentrate on the words, tone, and emotions being conveyed.

5. Mindful Driving:

- While driving, be fully present. Pay attention to the road, the feel of the steering wheel in your hands, and the sensation of your foot on the pedal. Avoid distractions like texting or daydreaming.

6. Mindful Showering:

- Use your daily shower as a mindfulness exercise. Feel the water on your skin, the temperature, and the sound it makes. Let go of worries and focus on the sensation of being cleansed and refreshed.

7. Mindful Cleaning:

- Turn household chores into mindful activities. Pay attention to the movements and sensations involved in cleaning. Feel the textures, smells, and visual details of the objects you're cleaning.

8. Mindful Work:

- In a work environment, practice mindfulness by concentrating fully on one task at a time. Minimize multitasking, and immerse yourself in the current project. Take breaks to reset and refocus.

9. Mindful Waiting:

- Use waiting time, whether in line or at an appointment, as an opportunity to practice mindfulness. Take a few moments to observe your surroundings, your breath, and the sensations in your body.

10. Mindful Technology Use: Be mindful of your technology consumption. Set aside specific times for checking emails, social media, or using your smartphone. Avoid constant checking and notifications that can lead to distraction and stress.

11. Mindful Relaxation: When you relax or unwind, be fully present in the moment. Whether you're reading, listening to music, or simply sitting quietly, immerse yourself in the experience without thinking about past or future concerns.

12. Mindful Self-Care: During self-care activities like taking a bath, meditating, or practicing yoga, focus entirely on the sensations and emotions involved. Let go of external distractions and judgments.

13. Mindful Gratitude: Regularly take time to reflect on the things you're grateful for. This can be done during a dedicated mindfulness practice or simply by acknowledging these things throughout the day.

14. Mindful Breathing Breaks: Take short mindfulness breaks throughout the day. Pause, take a few deep breaths, and center yourself. This can help you reset and reduce stress in hectic moments.

Remember that mindfulness is about being kind and non-judgmental toward yourself. It's normal for your mind to wander; when it does, gently bring your focus back to the present moment. Over time, practicing mindfulness in everyday activities can become a natural and enriching part of your life, enhancing your overall sense of well-being.

- **Finding inspiration through reading and self-reflection**

Finding inspiration through reading and self-reflection is a powerful way to stimulate personal growth, creativity, and a deeper understanding of yourself and the world around you. Here are some strategies for effectively using reading and self-reflection as sources of inspiration:

1. Diverse Reading Material:

- Expand your reading repertoire to include a variety of genres, topics, and perspectives. Fiction, non-fiction, biographies, self-help, philosophy, and poetry can all offer unique insights and inspiration.

2. Keep a Journal:

- Maintain a journal or diary where you can record your thoughts, ideas, and reflections. This practice can help you clarify your thoughts and track your personal growth over time.

3. Set Aside Quiet Time:

- Create a dedicated space and time for reading and self-reflection. It could be early in the morning, during your lunch break, or before bedtime. Consistency is key.

4. Mindful Reading:

- Approach your reading with mindfulness. Pay close attention to the words, concepts, and emotions evoked by the text. Take your time to savor and absorb the material.

5. Annotate and Highlight:

- While reading, underline or highlight passages that resonate with you. Jot down notes in the margins or in a separate notebook. This helps you engage more deeply with the material.

6. Discuss and Share:

- Engage in discussions about what you're reading. Share your thoughts and insights with friends, book clubs, or online communities. Hearing different perspectives can spark new ideas.

7. Seek Recommendations:

- Ask others for book recommendations or explore reading lists curated by experts or influencers in areas of interest. A well-chosen book can lead to profound inspiration.

8. Reflect on Personal Experiences:

- As you read, relate the material to your own experiences and challenges. Consider how the lessons or stories can be applied to your life.

9. Explore Different Cultures:

- Read literature and works from different cultures and backgrounds. This broadens your perspective and exposes you to diverse worldviews.

10. Set Goals and Take Action: Use your readings and reflections as a source of motivation. Set personal goals based on the insights you gain and take concrete steps toward achieving them.

11. Experiment with Writing: Use writing as a form of self-reflection. Journaling, poetry, and personal essays can help you explore your thoughts and feelings more deeply.

12. Practice Gratitude: Incorporate gratitude into your self-reflection. Reflect on the things you're grateful for in your life. This can lead to a more positive and inspired outlook.

13. Embrace Solitude: Find moments of solitude for deeper self-reflection. Whether through meditation, nature walks, or simply sitting in quiet contemplation, solitude can foster inspiration.

14. Be Patient: Inspiration doesn't always strike immediately. Sometimes, it takes time for the ideas and insights from your reading and self-reflection to coalesce into something meaningful.

15. Explore Multiple Perspectives: Challenge your existing beliefs and assumptions by reading material that presents different viewpoints. This can lead to personal growth and expanded horizons.

16. Practice Active Listening: In addition to reading, actively listen to podcasts, interviews, and lectures on topics that interest you. Hearing the spoken word can offer a different dimension of inspiration.

17. Connect with Others: Engage in meaningful conversations with people who share your interests or passions. Collaborative discussions can lead to creative breakthroughs.

18. Reflect on Your Values: Use self-reflection to clarify your values and priorities. Aligning your life choices with your values can be a powerful source of inspiration.

Remember that inspiration can come from unexpected places, so stay open to new ideas and experiences. By integrating reading and self-reflection into your daily routine, you can tap into a continuous wellspring of inspiration that enriches your life and fuels your personal and creative growth.

Chapter 9
Connecting with Others

- **Strategies for making new friends and strengthening existing connections**

Building and maintaining meaningful friendships is essential for emotional well-being and a fulfilling life. Here are strategies for making new friends and strengthening existing connections:

For Making New Friends:

1. Pursue Shared Interests:

- Join clubs, groups, or organizations that align with your interests. Whether it's a book club, a sports league, or a hobby group, shared activities provide opportunities to meet like-minded people.

2. Attend Social Events:

- Attend parties, gatherings, and events in your community. Be open to striking up conversations with new people. Networking events and social gatherings can be great for expanding your social circle.

3. Volunteer:

- Volunteering for a cause you care about is an excellent way to meet people who share your values and passions. It also provides a sense of purpose and fulfillment.

4. Take Classes:

- Enroll in classes or workshops that interest you, whether it's cooking, art, dance, or a language. Learning together creates natural bonding opportunities.

5. Online Communities:

- Participate in online forums, social media groups, or apps focused on your hobbies or interests. Engage in conversations and consider transitioning online connections to in-person meetups.

6. Be a Good Listener:

- When meeting new people, listen actively and show genuine interest in their stories and experiences. People appreciate good listeners and are more likely to want to connect with them.

7. Use Existing Connections:

- Ask your current friends to introduce you to their friends or social circles. Mutual connections can be an excellent way to expand your network.

8. Attend Meetup Groups:

- Explore meetup.com or similar platforms to find local groups and events centered around various interests, from outdoor activities to intellectual discussions.

9. Be Approachable:

- Smile, maintain open body language, and make eye contact when meeting new people. Approachability can make it easier for others to initiate conversations with you.

10. Be Patient: Building deep friendships takes time. Don't rush the process; focus on developing genuine connections rather than quantity.

For Strengthening Existing Connections:

1. Regular Communication:

- Make an effort to stay in touch with your friends through calls, texts, or video chats. Consistent communication helps maintain and strengthen bonds.

2. Plan Get-Togethers:

- Initiate plans to meet up with friends. Whether it's a casual coffee date, a movie night, or a weekend getaway, spending quality time together reinforces your connection.

3. Show Appreciation:

- Express gratitude and appreciation for your friends. A heartfelt message or a small gesture can go a long way in nurturing your relationships.

4. Be a Supportive Friend:

- Be there for your friends during their ups and downs. Offer a listening ear, empathy, and support when they need it most.

5. Create Shared Experiences:

- Create new memories together by trying new activities, going on adventures, or pursuing shared interests.

6. Respect Boundaries:

- Recognize and respect your friends' boundaries and personal space. Give them room to grow and evolve individually.

7. Apologize and Forgive:

- If conflicts or misunderstandings arise, be willing to apologize and forgive. Healthy friendships require the ability to resolve differences.

8. Be Reliable:

- Be a friend who can be counted on. Honor your commitments and be dependable in times of need.

9. Prioritize Friendships:

- Make an effort to prioritize your friendships amidst the demands of life. Nurture these relationships as you would any other important aspect of your life.

10. Be Yourself: Authenticity is key to maintaining lasting friendships. Be true to yourself, and let your friends do the same.

Remember that friendships require effort and nurturing. It's essential to invest time and energy into both making new friends and strengthening existing connections. Building meaningful relationships can contribute significantly to your overall happiness and well-being.

- **The role of social engagement in retirement**

Social engagement plays a pivotal role in retirement, contributing significantly to a retiree's overall well-being, happiness, and quality of life. Here's a detailed exploration of the importance and benefits of social engagement during retirement:

1. Combatting Loneliness:

- Retirement can sometimes lead to feelings of isolation and loneliness, especially if one loses the social interactions that work provides. Social engagement helps combat these feelings by providing regular opportunities for interaction and connection.

2. Emotional Support:

- Maintaining an active social life means having a support network in place. Friends and social connections can offer emotional support during life's challenges, providing a sense of belonging and security.

3. Cognitive Stimulation:

- Engaging in conversations, debates, and social activities keeps your mind sharp and active. It stimulates cognitive functions and can reduce the risk of cognitive decline.

4. Sense of Purpose:

- Social engagement provides a sense of purpose and responsibility. Being part of social groups or volunteering can give retirees a reason to get out of bed in the morning and contribute to their communities.

5. Physical Health:

- Socializing often involves physical activities, whether it's walking with a friend, dancing, or playing sports. These activities promote physical health, reduce the risk of chronic illnesses, and improve overall well-being.

6. Mental Health:

- Active social engagement has been linked to improved mental health. It can reduce symptoms of anxiety and depression and enhance overall emotional well-being.

7. Lifelong Learning:

- Social interactions provide opportunities for learning and personal growth. Engaging with people from diverse backgrounds exposes retirees to new ideas, perspectives, and experiences.

8. Friendship and Camaraderie:

- Building and maintaining friendships in retirement can bring immense joy and companionship. Sharing life experiences, hobbies, and interests with friends creates lasting bonds.

9. Active Lifestyle:

- Social engagements often involve physical activities, which encourage retirees to stay active and maintain a healthy lifestyle. From group fitness classes to outdoor adventures, staying social can mean staying fit.

10. Opportunities for Travel: Many retirees use their newfound free time to travel. Social engagement opens doors to group travel opportunities, allowing retirees to explore new destinations with friends and like-minded individuals.

11. Sense of Community: Being socially engaged fosters a sense of belonging to a larger community. Whether it's a neighborhood, religious group, or hobby club, retirees often find a supportive community in their social circles.

12. Connection to Younger Generations: Social engagement can involve interactions with younger generations, including grandchildren and local youth. These connections offer a chance for retirees to share wisdom and experiences.

13. Meaningful Retirement: Retirement isn't just about ceasing work; it's an opportunity to redefine one's life and find new meaning. Social engagement can provide retirees with a sense of purpose and fulfillment in this new chapter.

14. Lifelong Learning: Social interactions often lead to discussions and debates, encouraging continued learning and intellectual growth.

15. Celebrating Milestones: Social engagement ensures that retirees have a supportive network to celebrate birthdays, anniversaries, and other milestones, making these moments even more special.

In summary, social engagement is not just a pleasant aspect of retirement but a fundamental element that contributes to a fulfilling and healthy post-work life. It promotes emotional, physical, and mental well-being, keeps retirees active and engaged, and ensures that retirement is a time of joy, companionship, and personal growth. Building and maintaining social connections should be a central focus for retirees looking to make the most of this life stage.

- **The benefits of community involvement and volunteer work**

Community involvement and volunteer work offer numerous benefits, not only to the communities being served but also to the individuals who volunteer their time and effort. Here are some of the key advantages of community involvement and volunteer work:

1. Sense of Purpose and Fulfillment:

- Volunteering gives individuals a sense of purpose and fulfillment, as it allows them to make a positive impact on the lives of others. Contributing to a cause or community provides a deep sense of meaning.

2. Enhanced Well-Being:

- Studies have shown that volunteer work is associated with improved mental and emotional well-being. It can reduce symptoms of depression and anxiety, increase happiness, and boost self-esteem.

3. Social Connections:

- Volunteering is an excellent way to build and strengthen social connections. It provides opportunities to meet like-minded people and develop meaningful friendships.

4. Skill Development:

- Many volunteer roles require specific skills or offer opportunities for skill development. Volunteering can be a valuable way to gain new skills, enhance existing ones, and build a diverse skill set.

5. Increased Empathy and Compassion:

- Working with diverse groups of people and communities fosters empathy and compassion. Volunteers often develop a deeper understanding of others' struggles and challenges.

6. Networking and Professional Development:

- Volunteering can be a form of networking and professional development. It allows individuals to connect with others in their field, gain relevant experience, and enhance their resumes.

7. Improved Health:

- Volunteering has been linked to better physical health. Engaging in regular volunteer activities can reduce stress, lower blood pressure, and promote overall well-being.

8. Civic Engagement:

- Volunteer work fosters a sense of civic engagement and responsibility. It encourages individuals to actively participate in their communities and advocate for positive change.

9. Sense of Belonging:

- Community involvement provides a sense of belonging and connection to a larger group or cause. This can help combat feelings of isolation and loneliness.

10. Personal Growth: Volunteer work often challenges individuals to step out of their comfort zones and take on new responsibilities. This can lead to personal growth and increased self-confidence.

11. Impact on Community: Volunteer efforts contribute to the betterment of communities. Whether it's assisting vulnerable populations, supporting local organizations, or participating in environmental initiatives, volunteers play a vital role in creating positive change.

12. Lifelong Learning: Volunteering offers opportunities for continuous learning and personal development. Volunteers gain knowledge about social issues, cultures, and the needs of their communities.

13. Legacy Building: Many volunteers see their work as a way to leave a positive legacy for future generations. It's a way to make a lasting impact on the world.

14. Altruism and Giving Back: Volunteering allows individuals to practice altruism and giving back to society. It reinforces the idea of being part of a larger community and working together for the common good.

15. Strengthened Relationships: For families and couples, volunteering together can strengthen relationships and create shared experiences. It provides opportunities for bonding and teamwork.

16. Personal Satisfaction: Ultimately, volunteer work provides personal satisfaction and a sense of accomplishment. Knowing that you've made a difference in someone's life or in your community is a rewarding experience.

In summary, community involvement and volunteer work offer a wide range of benefits that extend beyond the act of giving. These activities can have a positive impact on mental and physical well-being, foster social connections, and provide opportunities for personal growth and development. Engaging in volunteer work is not only a way to give back to society but also a means of enriching one's own life.

- **Identifying opportunities to contribute to society**

Identifying opportunities to contribute to society can be a fulfilling and purpose-driven endeavor. Here are some strategies to help you find meaningful ways to make a positive impact:

1. Identify Your Passions and Interests:

- Start by reflecting on your passions and interests. What causes or issues resonate with you? Your commitment to a cause is more likely to be sustained if it aligns with your personal interests.

2. Assess Your Skills and Talents:

- Consider your skills, talents, and expertise. What are you good at, and how can you use these abilities to benefit others? Whether it's teaching, writing, organizing, or technical skills, your talents can be valuable.

3. Research Local Needs:

- Look into the needs of your local community. Reach out to local nonprofits, community organizations, or government agencies to understand the challenges they face and where volunteers or contributions are needed.

4. Explore National and International Causes:

- If you're interested in larger-scale or global issues, explore opportunities to contribute to national or international organizations. Many international NGOs and charities welcome volunteers and donors.

5. Connect with Existing Organizations:

- Consider joining existing organizations or groups dedicated to causes you care about. These organizations often have established ways for individuals to get involved, whether through volunteering, fundraising, or advocacy.

6. Volunteer Your Time:

- Volunteering is one of the most direct ways to contribute to society. Look for volunteer opportunities at local schools, hospitals, shelters, environmental organizations, or cultural institutions.

7. Share Your Knowledge:

- If you have expertise in a particular field, consider sharing your knowledge through mentoring, teaching, or workshops. Educational institutions and nonprofits often welcome experienced individuals as mentors or guest speakers.

8. Support Charitable Causes:

- Financial contributions to charitable organizations can have a significant impact. Research reputable charities and donate to causes you believe in.

9. Fundraise for a Cause:

- Organize fundraising events or campaigns for a specific cause. Whether it's a charity run, a bake sale, or an online crowdfunding campaign, fundraising can be a powerful way to make a difference.

10. Start Your Initiative: If you identify a gap or a need that isn't currently being addressed, consider starting your own initiative or nonprofit organization. It's a more significant commitment but can be incredibly rewarding.

11. Use Your Professional Skills: If you have specialized professional skills (e.g., legal, medical, marketing), consider offering pro bono services to individuals or organizations in need.

12. Engage in Advocacy and Awareness: Advocate for causes you're passionate about by raising awareness and mobilizing support. This can include writing articles, speaking at events, or using social media to spread the word.

13. Participate in Community Cleanups: Join or organize community cleanups to improve the environment in your neighborhood or city.

14. Support Local Businesses and Artisans: Buy from local businesses and artisans, which can help boost your community's economy and support small entrepreneurs.

15. Encourage Civic Engagement: Encourage others to become involved in contributing to society. Lead by example and inspire friends and family to join you in making a positive impact.

16. Stay Informed: Stay informed about current events, societal issues, and emerging needs. Being aware of evolving challenges can help you identify new opportunities to contribute.

17. Seek Feedback: Continuously seek feedback from the organizations or individuals you're assisting. This allows you to refine your contributions and make a more meaningful impact.

Remember that contributing to society doesn't always require a significant time commitment or financial resources. Small acts of kindness, volunteer efforts, and advocacy can collectively lead to positive change. The key is to find a cause or approach that resonates with you personally, as this will sustain your commitment and passion for making a difference.

Chapter 10
Crafting Your Retirement Legacy

- **Reflecting on your life's purpose and legacy**

Reflecting on your life's purpose and legacy is a profound and introspective journey that can bring clarity, meaning, and direction to your life. Here's a step-by-step guide to help you explore and define your life's purpose and legacy:

1. Self-Reflection:

- Begin by setting aside dedicated time for self-reflection. Find a quiet, comfortable space where you can think deeply about your life.

2. Contemplate Your Values:

- Consider the values that are most important to you. What principles guide your decisions and actions? Your values often provide clues about your life's purpose.

3. Explore Your Passions:

- Reflect on your passions and interests. What activities or pursuits bring you the most joy and fulfillment? Passion can be a strong indicator of your life's purpose.

4. Identify Your Strengths:

- Recognize your strengths, talents, and skills. What are you naturally good at, and how can you use these abilities to make a positive impact?

5. Reflect on Past Experiences:

- Think about the significant experiences, challenges, and achievements in your life. What have you learned from these experiences, and how have they shaped your values and goals?

6. Consider What Inspires You:

- Identify people, books, role models, or experiences that inspire you. What is it about them that resonates with you, and how can you incorporate those elements into your life's purpose?

7. Define Your Legacy:

- Imagine how you want to be remembered by your loved ones, your community, and the world. What kind of impact do you want to leave behind? What legacy do you aspire to create?

8. Set Goals and Priorities:

- Based on your reflections, set specific, actionable goals that align with your life's purpose and legacy. Break these goals down into manageable steps.

9. Live with Intention:

- Incorporate your life's purpose into your daily life. Make intentional choices that reflect your values and contribute to your legacy. Live in alignment with your goals.

10. Seek Guidance and Support: Discuss your reflections and goals with trusted friends, family members, or a mentor. They can offer valuable insights and encouragement.

11. Embrace Growth and Adaptation: Understand that your life's purpose and legacy may evolve over time. Be open to growth and adaptation as you gain new experiences and insights.

12. Take Action: Put your reflections into action by actively pursuing your goals and living according to your purpose. This may involve volunteering, starting a project, or making changes in your career or personal life.

13. Practice Gratitude: Regularly express gratitude for the opportunities and experiences that contribute to your purpose and legacy. Gratitude can deepen your sense of fulfillment.

14. Document Your Journey: Consider keeping a journal or creating a personal legacy document that records your reflections, goals, and actions. This can serve as a meaningful record of your life's purpose and legacy for future generations.

15. Leave a Positive Impact: Continuously strive to leave a positive impact on the lives of others and on the world. Your actions, kindness, and contributions can ripple outward, creating a lasting legacy.

16. Review and Adjust: Periodically review your life's purpose and legacy goals. Adjust them as needed to stay aligned with your evolving values and aspirations.

Remember that discovering your life's purpose and defining your legacy is a deeply personal and ongoing process. It may take time, and it's okay to revisit and refine your reflections as you grow and change. Ultimately, living with purpose and creating a meaningful legacy can bring a profound sense of fulfillment and leave a lasting positive impact on the world.

- ## How to create a meaningful retirement legacy?

Creating a meaningful retirement legacy involves intentionally planning and taking actions that leave a positive impact on the world, your community, and the people you care about. Here are steps to help you create a meaningful retirement legacy:

1. Define Your Values and Priorities:

- Start by reflecting on your core values and priorities. What matters most to you? What causes, issues, or areas do you want to focus on during your retirement years?

2. Identify Your Passions and Interests:

- Consider the activities and interests that bring you the most joy and fulfillment. Your passions can be a powerful driving force behind your retirement legacy.

3. Set Clear Goals and Objectives:

- Define specific goals and objectives for your retirement legacy. What impact do you want to make, and how do you envision achieving it?

4. Choose a Focus Area:

- Decide on a focus area or cause that aligns with your values and interests. It could be related to education, healthcare, the environment, social justice, or any other area you're passionate about.

5. Volunteer and Give Back:

- Dedicate time to volunteer work and philanthropy. Find organizations, charities, or causes that resonate with your chosen focus area and offer your time, skills, or financial support.

6. Mentor and Share Knowledge:

- Consider mentoring younger generations or individuals in your field of expertise. Sharing your knowledge and experiences can have a lasting impact on others.

7. Create a Legacy Project:

- Develop a specific legacy project or initiative that reflects your values and goals. This could involve starting a community program, supporting a local charity, or launching an educational project.

8. Collaborate and Build Partnerships:

- Collaborate with like-minded individuals, organizations, or community groups. Building partnerships can amplify your impact and create a network of support.

9. Document Your Journey:

- Keep a record of your legacy-building journey. This could include maintaining a journal, creating a website or blog, or producing videos that document your experiences and contributions.

10. Involve Your Family: Discuss your retirement legacy plans with your family and loved ones. Their support and involvement can be valuable, and it ensures that your legacy aligns with your family's values.

11. Focus on Sustainability: Consider the long-term sustainability of your legacy efforts. Aim to create initiatives or projects that can continue to thrive even after you're no longer actively involved.

12. Seek Professional Advice: If your legacy plans involve financial contributions or complex initiatives, consider consulting with financial advisors, lawyers, or experts in the relevant field to ensure your efforts are well-executed.

13. Review and Adapt: Periodically review your retirement legacy goals and adapt them as needed. Life circumstances and priorities may change, and your legacy should evolve accordingly.

14. Inspire and Engage Others: Use your retirement legacy as an opportunity to inspire and engage others to get involved in causes they are passionate about. Encourage your peers and the younger generation to make a positive impact.

15. Measure and Celebrate Your Impact: Regularly assess the impact of your retirement legacy initiatives. Celebrate milestones and achievements, and use the feedback to refine your efforts.

16. Leave a Personal Legacy: Beyond your contributions to causes and communities, consider the personal legacy you want to leave. This might involve leaving behind memoirs, family traditions, or cherished memories.

17. Consider Philanthropic Giving: If financially feasible, establish a charitable foundation, donate to causes you care about, or leave a significant portion of your estate to charitable organizations in your will.

18. Enjoy the Journey: Remember to enjoy the journey of building your retirement legacy. The fulfillment and joy you experience along the way are as important as the impact you make.

Creating a meaningful retirement legacy is about making a positive and lasting mark on the world while aligning your actions with your values and passions. It's a deeply rewarding and purposeful way to spend your retirement years, and it can leave a lasting positive impact on future generations.

Conclusion: Keep the Fun Rolling

As you reach the final chapter of "Retirement Fun 2024," we hope you've found inspiration and valuable insights that will guide you on your retirement journey. This book has been a roadmap to help you navigate the exciting adventure that is retirement. But remember, it's not the end of the road; it's the beginning of a new, vibrant chapter in your life.

Throughout these pages, we've explored the myriad ways you can create your own unique retirement experience. From envisioning your dream lifestyle to embracing new adventures, you've discovered the keys to making retirement your own. You've learned how to balance routine and spontaneity, pursue your passions, and find joy in both simple pleasures and grand adventures.

We've delved into the importance of staying physically active, maintaining strong social connections, and leaving a meaningful legacy. You've uncovered the power of mindfulness, self-reflection, and continuous learning to enrich your retirement years.

Now, as you approach this conclusion, we want to leave you with a final, heartfelt message: Keep the fun rolling.

Your retirement is an opportunity to do more of what you love, to savor life's pleasures, and to make a lasting impact on the world around you. It's a chance to redefine your purpose, set new goals, and live each day to the fullest. Whether you're traveling to far-flung destinations, volunteering in your community, pursuing creative passions, or simply savoring the serenity of nature, your retirement is your canvas to paint with the colors of joy and fulfillment.

Don't forget that the journey of retirement is as important as the destination. Embrace each moment, savor the experiences, and find joy in the everyday. Share your wisdom, your laughter, and your love with those around you. And as you create your own retirement legacy, remember that you have the power to shape a future that is meaningful, purposeful, and deeply satisfying.

As you close this book and step into your retirement adventure, we encourage you to define and pursue your version of fun with enthusiasm and vigor. Your retirement is a celebration of life's achievements and a Launchpad for new dreams. So, keep the fun rolling, and may your retirement be a journey filled with joy, fulfillment, and endless possibilities.

Congratulations on the exciting path that lies ahead, and may your retirement be a time of boundless happiness and unforgettable memories.

Here's to the fun, the adventure, and the joy of your retirement years. Cheers!

Appendix: Lists of Activities and Resources

Appendix A: Travel Destinations

Activities:

- Explore historical landmarks and museums.
- Take scenic drives through picturesque landscapes.
- Visit local markets and taste regional cuisine.
- Embark on hiking and nature trails.
- Attend cultural festivals and events.
- Enjoy water-based activities such as snorkeling, kayaking, or sailing.
- Participate in guided tours and workshops.
- Experience wildlife safaris and nature reserves.

Resources:

- Travel websites and blogs for destination inspiration.
- Travel agencies for planning and booking.
- Guidebooks and travel apps for tips and recommendations.
- Local tourism websites for up-to-date information.
- Online forums and social media groups for traveler insights.
- Travel insurance providers for peace of mind.

Appendix B: Stay-at-Home Activities

Activities:

1. **Reading**: Dive into a good book or explore various genres to expand your horizons.
2. **Cooking and Baking**: Experiment with new recipes and discover your culinary talents.
3. **Art and Craft Projects**: Explore your creativity through painting, drawing, knitting, or other crafts.
4. **Gardening**: Create a beautiful garden or nurture indoor plants for a sense of accomplishment.
5. **Home Improvement**: Tackle DIY home projects, redecorate rooms, or organize your living space.
6. **Online Learning**: Enroll in online courses or webinars to acquire new skills or knowledge.
7. **Yoga and Meditation**: Practice relaxation techniques to enhance your physical and mental well-being.

8. **Music**: Learn to play a musical instrument, explore music appreciation, or simply enjoy listening to your favorite tunes.
9. **Board Games and Puzzles**: Engage in board games, puzzles, or brain-teasers for mental stimulation.
10. **Movie and TV Show Marathons**: Catch up on movies and TV series you missed during your working years.
11. **Writing**: Start a journal, write short stories, or explore creative writing as a hobby.
12. **Virtual Tours**: Take virtual tours of museums, historical sites, and cultural attractions online.
13. **Photography**: Discover the art of photography by capturing moments and scenes around your home.
14. **Home-Based Exercise**: Establish a fitness routine with home workouts, yoga, or tai chi.
15. **DIY Projects**: Create handmade gifts, furniture, or decorative items for your home.
16. **Cooking Challenges**: Participate in cooking or baking challenges and share your creations with friends and family.
17. **Online Gaming**: Connect with friends or join online gaming communities for interactive fun.
18. **Genealogy Research**: Trace your family tree and uncover your ancestral history.
19. **Language Learning**: Master a new language or improve your proficiency in one you already know.
20. **Virtual Book Club**: Join or start a virtual book club to discuss literature with fellow enthusiasts.

Resources:

- Online cooking and recipe websites for culinary inspiration.
- Art supply stores or online retailers for art and craft materials.
- Gardening guides and tutorials for cultivating plants.
- Home improvement stores for tools and materials.
- Online learning platforms like Coursera, edX, or Khan Academy.
- Yoga and meditation apps or online classes.
- Musical instrument tutorials and sheet music resources.
- Board games and puzzles available for purchase online.
- Streaming platforms for movie and TV show access.
- Writing workshops or creative writing courses.
- Virtual tour websites for exploring destinations from home.
- Photography tutorials and editing software.
- Exercise and yoga video tutorials online.
- DIY project ideas and instructions from websites and books.
- Online gaming platforms and gaming communities.

- Genealogy research websites and archives.
- Language learning apps and online language courses.
- Online book clubs and reading groups.

These stay-at-home activities provide you with a wide range of options to keep yourself engaged, entertained, and mentally stimulated during your retirement. Enjoy exploring these activities and resources from the comfort of your home.

Appendix C: Outdoor Adventure Ideas

Outdoor Adventure Ideas:

1. **Hiking**: Explore nearby trails, nature reserves, and national parks.
2. **Camping**: Experience the great outdoors by camping in tents or cabins.
3. **Biking**: Discover scenic bike paths and trails in your area.
4. **Fishing**: Enjoy peaceful moments by the water while fishing.
5. **Canoeing or Kayaking**: Paddle down rivers, lakes, or calm waters.
6. **Birdwatching**: Observe and identify local bird species.
7. **Photography Expeditions**: Capture the beauty of nature through photography.
8. **Stargazing**: Set up a telescope and explore the night sky.
9. **Rock Climbing**: Challenge yourself with rock climbing adventures.
10. **Geocaching**: Embark on a modern-day treasure hunt with GPS devices.
11. **Wildlife Safari**: Go on wildlife tours to observe animals in their natural habitat.
12. **Zip Lining**: Experience an adrenaline rush with zip line adventures.
13. **Botanical Gardens**: Visit botanical gardens to admire diverse plant life.
14. **Beachcombing**: Search for seashells and treasures along the coastline.
15. **Horseback Riding**: Explore scenic trails on horseback.
16. **Hot Air Ballooning**: Soar above landscapes in a hot air balloon.
17. **Mountain Climbing**: Conquer summits and take in breathtaking vistas.
18. **Cave Exploration**: Explore caves and underground formations.
19. **Sailing or Boating**: Set sail on lakes or rivers.
20. **Whale Watching**: Join whale-watching tours to spot these majestic creatures.

Resources:

- Local hiking and outdoor clubs for group adventures.
- Camping gear and equipment rental stores.
- Bike shops for purchasing or renting bicycles.
- Fishing supply stores and local fishing regulations.
- Canoe and kayak rental companies.
- Birdwatching guidebooks and online forums.

- Photography workshops and nature photography guides.
- Astronomy clubs and stargazing apps.
- Rock climbing gyms and outdoor climbing guides.
- Geocaching websites and apps.
- Wildlife tour operators and national park guides.
- Zip lining companies and adventure parks.
- Botanical garden websites and local events.
- Beachcombing guides and coastal preservation groups.
- Horseback riding stables and trail guides.
- Hot air ballooning companies and festivals.
- Mountain climbing guides and safety courses.
- Cave exploration tours and caving organizations.
- Sailing and boating clubs or rental facilities.
- Whale watching tours and marine conservation groups.

These outdoor adventure ideas offer opportunities to connect with nature, challenge yourself, and create lasting memories during your retirement. Be sure to consider safety precautions and any necessary permits or equipment for each adventure. Enjoy the beauty of the great outdoors!

Appendix D: Exercise and Fitness Resources

Exercise and Fitness Activities:

1. **Walking**: Start with regular walks in your neighborhood or local parks.
2. **Running**: Begin a jogging routine to improve cardiovascular health.
3. **Cycling**: Ride a bike for low-impact cardiovascular exercise.
4. **Swimming**: Swim laps at a local pool for a full-body workout.
5. **Yoga**: Practice yoga to improve flexibility, balance, and mental well-being.
6. **Tai Chi**: Explore the graceful movements of tai chi for balance and relaxation.
7. **Strength Training**: Use resistance bands or free weights to build muscle.
8. **Pilates**: Develop core strength and flexibility through pilates workouts.
9. **Dancing**: Join dance classes or enjoy dancing at home for cardiovascular exercise.
10. **Aerobics**: Follow aerobic workout routines for a fun and energetic workout.
11. **Hiking**: Take on challenging hiking trails for endurance and leg strength.
12. **Swimming**: Swim laps at a local pool for a full-body workout.
13. **Group Fitness Classes**: Attend group fitness classes at a gym or online.
14. **Martial Arts**: Learn martial arts for physical fitness and self-defense.
15. **Gardening**: Engage in gardening activities for strength and flexibility.
16. **Outdoor Sports**: Play sports like tennis, golf, or pickleball for fitness and fun.
17. **Circuit Training**: Create your circuit training routine to target different muscle groups.

18. **Rowing**: Use a rowing machine for a full-body, low-impact workout.
19. **Water Aerobics**: Join water aerobics classes for gentle resistance training.
20. **Stretching**: Incorporate daily stretching exercises for flexibility and relaxation.

Resources:

- Fitness apps and websites for workout routines and tracking progress.
- Local gyms, fitness centers, and personal trainers for guidance.
- Yoga studios or online platforms for yoga classes.
- Tai chi classes or instructional videos.
- Strength training guides and workout plans.
- Pilates studios or online classes.
- Dance studios or dance workout videos.
- Aerobic workout videos and classes.
- Hiking trails and outdoor adventure groups.
- Martial arts schools or online martial arts courses.
- Gardening tips and community gardening programs.
- Sports clubs or local recreational leagues.
- Circuit training guides and equipment.
- Rowing machine tutorials and workouts.
- Water aerobics classes at local pools.
- Stretching routines and flexibility guides.

These exercise and fitness resources offer a wide range of options to stay active and maintain physical health during retirement. Whether you prefer solo activities or group classes, there are plenty of opportunities to incorporate exercise into your daily routine and lead a healthier lifestyle.

Appendix E: Soul-Nourishing Activities

Soul-Nourishing Activities:

1. **Meditation**: Practice mindfulness and meditation for inner peace and mental clarity.
2. **Journaling**: Keep a journal to reflect on your thoughts, experiences, and emotions.
3. **Nature Walks**: Take leisurely walks in nature to connect with the outdoors.
4. **Mindful Breathing**: Engage in deep, mindful breathing exercises for relaxation.
5. **Art Therapy**: Express yourself through art, such as drawing, painting, or sculpting.
6. **Music Therapy**: Listen to soothing or uplifting music to enhance your mood.
7. **Reading**: Immerse yourself in books that inspire, comfort, or challenge your thinking.
8. **Volunteering**: Dedicate time to volunteer for causes that align with your values.
9. **Spiritual Practices**: Explore and nurture your spiritual beliefs and practices.
10. **Gratitude Journaling**: Write down daily expressions of gratitude to foster positivity.

11. **Mindful Eating**: Savor each bite during meals, practicing mindful eating.
12. **Forest Bathing**: Immerse yourself in the healing energies of forests.
13. **Stargazing**: Spend time observing the night sky and contemplating the cosmos.
14. **Yoga Retreats**: Attend yoga retreats for holistic well-being and self-discovery.
15. **Soulful Conversations**: Engage in deep, meaningful conversations with loved ones.
16. **Candlelight Meditation**: Meditate by candlelight for a calming atmosphere.
17. **Labyrinth Walks**: Experience the meditative benefits of walking labyrinths.
18. **Connecting with Pets**: Bond with and care for pets for companionship and joy.
19. **Feng Shui**: Create harmonious living spaces with Feng Shui principles.
20. **Digital Detox**: Unplug from screens periodically for mental clarity and presence.

Resources:

- Meditation apps and guided meditation recordings.
- Journals, notebooks, and writing prompts for journaling.
- Nature trails, parks, and botanical gardens for walks.
- Breathing exercises and relaxation techniques guides.
- Art supplies and online art classes.
- Music streaming platforms and playlists for relaxation.
- Libraries and bookstores for a wide selection of reading materials.
- Volunteer organizations and local community programs.
- Places of worship and spiritual communities.
- Gratitude journaling prompts and templates.
- Mindful eating resources and mindful meal guides.
- Forest bathing resources and guided experiences.
- Telescopes and astronomy clubs for stargazing.
- Yoga retreat centers and online yoga workshops.
- Conversation starters for meaningful discussions.
- Candles and candlelight meditation instructions.
- Labyrinth locations and resources.
- Pet adoption centers and pet care resources.
- Feng Shui books and consultants.
- Digital detox strategies and mindful tech usage tips.

These soul-nourishing activities and resources provide opportunities for self-discovery, inner peace, and a deeper connection with yourself and the world around you. Consider incorporating these activities into your daily or weekly routine to enhance your overall well-being during retirement.

Appendix F: Community Engagement and Volunteering Opportunities

Community Engagement and Volunteering Opportunities:

1. **Mentoring**: Offer your knowledge and guidance to mentor younger generations.
2. **Tutoring**: Assist students with their academic pursuits and homework.
3. **Senior Companionship**: Provide companionship and support to fellow seniors.
4. **Local Libraries**: Volunteer at libraries to promote literacy and reading.
5. **Hospital Volunteering**: Offer comfort and assistance to patients and their families.
6. **Homeless Shelters**: Volunteer at shelters to help those in need.
7. **Food Banks**: Support food banks by sorting, packing, or distributing food.
8. **Environmental Cleanup**: Join efforts to clean up parks, beaches, or natural areas.
9. **Animal Shelters**: Care for and assist with the adoption of animals in shelters.
10. **Community Gardens**: Participate in community gardening projects.
11. **Youth Programs**: Get involved in youth programs and after-school activities.
12. **Community Centers**: Assist with programs and events at local community centers.
13. **Disaster Relief**: Volunteer for disaster relief organizations.
14. **Hospice Care**: Offer comfort and companionship to hospice patients.
15. **Crisis Helplines**: Provide support to individuals in crisis via phone or chat.
16. **Arts and Culture**: Contribute to arts and cultural organizations and events.
17. **Community Events**: Assist with organizing and running community events.
18. **Environmental Advocacy**: Advocate for environmental protection and conservation.
19. **Human Rights**: Get involved in human rights organizations and causes.
20. **International Volunteering**: Explore opportunities for global volunteering.

Resources:

- Volunteer organizations and databases for finding opportunities.
- Local schools, libraries, and community centers for tutoring and mentoring.
- Senior centers and retirement communities for companionship programs.
- Libraries for literacy programs and reading assistance.
- Hospitals and healthcare facilities for volunteer programs.
- Homeless shelters and outreach organizations for volunteer roles.
- Food banks and food rescue organizations for volunteering.
- Environmental groups and park services for cleanup events.
- Animal shelters and rescue organizations for volunteering.
- Community garden associations and local gardening clubs.
- Youth programs, schools, and sports clubs for youth engagement.
- Community centers and their program coordinators for volunteer positions.
- Disaster relief organizations and training programs.

- Hospice care centers and hospice volunteer training.
- Crisis helplines and crisis intervention training.
- Local arts organizations and cultural events coordinators.
- Community event organizers and planning committees.
- Environmental advocacy groups and local initiatives.
- Human rights organizations and advocacy campaigns.
- International volunteer organizations and opportunities.

Engaging with your community and volunteering your time and skills can be immensely rewarding during retirement. These opportunities allow you to make a positive impact, connect with others, and contribute to causes that matter to you. Explore the options in your area and find a fulfilling way to give back to your community.

Printed in Great Britain
by Amazon